Lesson Planning Tweaks for Teachers

Other titles available from Bloomsbury Education:

100 Ideas for Secondary Teachers: Outstanding English Lessons by Angella Cooze and Mary Myatt
100 Ideas for Secondary Teachers: Outstanding Lessons by Ross Morrison McGill
100 Ideas for Secondary Teachers: Outstanding Mathematics Lessons by Mike Ollerton
How to Survive an Ofsted Inspection by Sarah Findlater
The Spider Strategy by Marcella McCarthy
Secondary Starters and Plenaries by Kate Brown

Lesson Planning Tweaks for Teachers

Small changes that make a big difference!

Melanie Aberson & Debbie Light

B L O O M S B U R Y

LONDON • OXFORD • NEW YORK • NEW DELHI • SYDNEY

Bloomsbury Education

An imprint of Bloomsbury Publishing Plc

50 Bedford Square   1385 Broadway
London   New York
WC1B 3DP   NY 10018
UK   USA

www.bloomsbury.com

Bloomsbury is a registered trade mark of Bloomsbury Publishing Plc

First published 2015

© Melanie Aberson and Debbie Light 2015

British Library Cataloguing-in-Publication Data

A catalogue record for this book is available from the British Library.

ISBN: PB: 9781472916150
ePub: 9781472916174
ePDF: 9781472916167

Library of Congress Cataloging-in-Publication Data

A catalog record for this book is available from the Library of Congress.

10 9 8 7 6 5 4 3 2

Typeset by Newgen Knowledge Works (P) Ltd., Chennai, India
Printed and bound by CPI Group (UK) Ltd, Croydon, CR0 4YY

This book is produced using paper that is made from wood grown in managed, sustainable forests. It is natural, renewable and recyclable. The logging and manufacturing processes conform to the environmental regulations of the country of origin.

To view more of our titles please visit www.bloomsbury.com

Online resources accompany this book at:
www.bloomsbury.com/lesson-planning-tweaks

Please type the URL into your web browser and follow the instructions to access the resources. If you experience any problems, please contact Bloomsbury at: companionwebsite@bloomsbury.com

Contents

Acknowledgements vii

Introduction 1

How to use this book 4

1   An introduction to lesson planning 6

Our lesson plans 7
The formal lesson plan 8
The one page plan 9
Planning a lesson 18

2   Assessment for Learning 19

Constructing and sharing challenging learning intentions 19
Modelling and sharing high-quality exemplars 23
Peer feedback 26
Reviewing learning 29
Annotated History lesson plan 32
Annotated Media arts lesson plan 36
Top tweaks checklist: AfL 40
Learning leader: AfL 41

3   Questioning 43

Questioning to encourage pupils to think deeply 43
Questioning to check understanding 47
Questioning to reflect and review progress 50
Peer-to-peer questioning 53
Annotated Design and technology lesson plan 56
Annotated English lesson plan 60
Top tweaks checklist: questioning 64
Learning leader: questioning 65

4   Stretch and challenge 67

Grouping strategies 68
Provision of choices 71
Developing independence 75
Collaborative learning 78

Annotated Business studies lesson plan 82
Annotated PE lesson plan 86
Top tweaks checklist: stretch and challenge 89
Learning leader: stretch and challenge 90

5 Commitment to learning 91

Dealing with getting stuck 91
Growth mindset 95
Creating a culture of excellence 98
Ability to listen to and learn from their peers 102
Annotated Art and design lesson plan 106
Annotated Religious education lesson plan 110
Top tweaks checklist: commitment to learning 114
Learning leader: commitment to learning 115

6 Marking and feedback 117

Tweaking your marking and feedback planning 120
Top tweaks checklist: marking and feedback 124
Learning leader: marking and feedback 125

References 127
Appendices 129
Subject index 133
Index 135

Acknowledgements

We would both like to thank the amazing teachers we have been fortunate to work with during our careers. Between us we have observed hundreds of lessons and these have given us ideas for this book, but more importantly the inspiration to become better teachers. Many talented colleagues gave us permission to use their lesson plans and ideas and we would particularly like to thank Chris Seymour, Michelle Buckley, Michael O'Neill, Deborah Yates, Jamie Black, Emma Wyatt and Jessica Dewes. We would also like to thank our schools, Drayton Manor High School and Elthorne Park High School, for giving us the opportunity and time to work together and with others to develop our ideas and for encouraging us to blog about our experiences as teachers and leaders. This book is a compilation of ideas we have developed over the years and wonderful things we have discovered online. We have tried out best to really carefully reference all of the ideas and strategies we mention in this book, but due to the fantastic world of sharing resources on Twitter there may be an idea, activity or strategy that we mention that we have not referenced correctly. If this is the case, please do contact us and we will rectify!

Since joining Twitter we have been overwhelmed by the kindness of teachers we hardly know! There are a wealth of ideas available through Twitter but it provides much more than that; it is a community of reflective and proactive teachers. There is always someone who will help you out when you need a resource, an opinion, idea or suggestion or just pointing in a particular direction. We would like to thank those online colleagues who agreed to read the book and provide initial feedback: Stephen Tierney, the wonderful @LeadingLearner who has the most energising positivity; Zoe Elder, @fullonlearning, who gave us reassurance and excellent advice and Jill Berry, @jillberry102, who read the book so carefully and even took the time to correct our grammar (once an English teacher, always an English teacher!). These people must be busier than we can imagine, but made the time for us and we will be forever grateful.

Most of all we must also thank our long-suffering families for putting up with two teachers who are a little bit too obsessed with teaching and learning.

Debbie: I'd like to thank my husband Rob for agreeing to lose me for one summer to write the first draft of the book and for putting up with my Twitter addiction. Also, I'd like to thank my mum and dad for always supporting me and believing I can do anything if I put my mind to it.

Melanie: Thanks to my fiancé Ross, who knows much more about teaching than any non-teacher would ever want to, my sister Steph and my mum Jean, who tried to give me a realistic view of the teaching profession. Special thanks to my wonderful dad Johan, who painstakingly and forensically edited the first draft of this book. I love you all and Dad, I hope you get to see the final version.

Introduction

We decided to write this book after undergoing an Ofsted inspection together as Advanced Skills Teachers. In recent versions of the Ofsted framework, there is an increased focus on learning and teaching. Gone are the days when a school could be given an overall judgement of outstanding without being given the same grading for quality of teaching. Our school moved from a 2 grading to a 1 for quality of teaching, giving us an overall judgement of outstanding. It is no coincidence that, since the last Ofsted inspection, the school has put a significant emphasis on the areas we are discussing in this book. The majority of our CPD has been focused on learning and teaching, which has led to much more discussion amongst staff about what they are trying out with their pupils. Even though we do not work in the same school any more, we still believe that the schools we now work in will only be truly outstanding if there is an embedded culture where best practice is explored and developed in a variety of formats, be it action research, lesson study, staff bulletins and blogs, departmental training, peer coaching or book clubs.

In our experience, teachers are constantly thinking about how they can make the learning experience better for their pupils. Having observed a plethora of lessons across different subject areas in several schools, and delivered extensive training, we believe that the majority of teachers just need to 'tweak' rather than reinvent the proverbial wheel. Recently, there has been much debate surrounding the so-called outstanding lesson. There have been too many awful anecdotes from teachers about their experience of being observed by either their line manager or an Ofsted inspector, who have failed to gain that elusive outstanding grade because of the most ridiculous of reasons. Thankfully, there has been a groundswell in abandoning this absurd pursuit of the outstanding lesson and a greater focus on delivering quality lessons every day that leads to outstanding learning over time.

Professor Rob Coe (2013), after analysing extensive research, has argued convincingly that grading individual lessons is pretty much pointless because observers' judgements are so often wrong and far too subjective. In 2014, Ofsted published a report from the director of schools at the time, Mike Cladingbowl, where it stated clearly that individual lessons should not be graded and inspectors should focus more on teaching and learning over time. In the current Ofsted framework, it is now made explicit that Ofsted will make a judgement on the quality of teaching which is based on a range of sources including lesson observations, work scrutiny, student interviews and progress data. Using a broader range of evidence should lead to more accurate judgements on the quality of teaching.

Although this change in focus has been welcomed by the majority of the teaching profession, it does mean that there is a lot more pressure on teachers to develop their teaching. The one-off jazz hands observation lesson where you stick in every gimmick you've ever heard of so you can be given an outstanding grading just isn't going to cut it anymore. If it's all about progress over time then teachers need to carefully consider what they teach, how they teach and why they have decided to teach in this way. The routines that teachers set up in their classrooms and are embedded over time will make the real difference. We want to stress that, although you will see individual teacher's lesson plans in this book, these teachers are great teachers because this is how they teach **all** of the time – not just when they are being observed. Our profession has been bogged down by countless initiatives, policies and buzz words that mean teachers can end up seeing teaching as a tick-box exercise, rather than getting to the core of what excellent learning and teaching is all about.

Regardless of what initiative is given priority at the moment, an outstanding teacher is fairly easy to spot and this is how:

- ***Outstanding teachers are open and reflective about their practice.*** They constantly talk about their lessons – even those that go wrong. When things go wrong, they focus on what they should do next, rather than apportioning blame; when things go right, they share their successes and resources to enable other colleagues to improve their practice. They believe in Dylan Wiliam's statement that 'Every teacher needs to improve, not because they are not good enough, but because they can be even better' (Wiliam, 2012). These teachers are on a constant quest of self-improvement, recognising that they have to take an active role in their own professional development. They make the most of training sessions, use social media such as Twitter to engage with other professionals and read blogs and books in their spare time. Being an outstanding teacher takes a lot of hard work; what you see happening in their classrooms doesn't just happen by accident.

- ***Outstanding teachers create lessons that allow all of their pupils to shine.*** The teacher's subject knowledge and experience is respected but outstanding teachers generally don't tend to set themselves up as the 'expert' with all of the answers; they use their expert knowledge effectively to explain and model new concepts and ideas to pupils, but they also invest time in demonstrating what it means to be a good learner. They encourage their pupils to ask questions, try things out and not be afraid to fail. A climate of trust is built in order for pupils to feel safe to take risks. These risks ultimately lead to them becoming better learners. When pupils feel like they have encountered something difficult and then persevered to gain a deeper understanding, this creates a sense of pride. Have the highest expectations of your pupils at all times and expect them to produce their best. Creating a culture in the classroom where everyone is striving to do their best takes time, but it's worth it.

- ***Outstanding teachers really know their pupils.*** Data is a useful starting point, but excellent teachers can see past the data. Outstanding teachers know the stories behind the data so they can pitch their lessons to ensure all pupils are appropriately challenged. They can identify patterns in the data that make them reflect on the lessons they have taught and whether their pupils have fully understood new ideas and concepts. They plan their questions to target different levels of ability and take the time to plan activities which will not only help the pupils make progress, but will also be engaging. The word 'engaging' has become a dirty word in some corners of the teaching profession, but it is not the same as 'gimmicky' or doing something fun without there being any real learning going on. On the other hand, there is a misconception amongst others in the profession that pupils will work harder if lessons are 'fun'. We don't think either of these limited perspectives is particularly helpful. For us, engaging your pupils means that the tasks you are asking them to work on are challenging, require a concerted effort and are wholly relevant to the new knowledge you want them to understand. Pupils can identify teachers who put in the extra effort to bring out the best in them. This effort is reflected in the supportive relationships between pupils and the teacher that can be seen clearly when entering the classroom.

So can anyone be outstanding? Yes – but not all of the time! In fact, if you're too focused on chasing the title of outstanding then this can create a negative impact on your teaching. Focus on improving your teaching for the benefit of the pupils in your classes, not for the looming presence of the inspector. There will always be lessons that make you cringe when you think back on them or even bring you out in a cold sweat. Don't dwell too much on these lessons; learn from them and move on. Sometimes things happen that are beyond your control. Even Ofsted inspectors recognise this (or so we're told . . .). The important thing is that teachers are flexible and can think on their feet. If things aren't working, change something. Don't flog to death a lesson plan that is just not working in practice.

How to use this book

This book provides real examples of lesson plans created by highly effective teachers. One of the common questions we get asked in our training is: 'How does this apply to my subject?' Consequently, we've tried to use lesson plans and lesson snippets from a range of subjects to show that our strategies can be employed throughout the curriculum. Having observed hundreds of lessons, we have seen countless examples of excellent practice so when choosing what to share in this book, we have thought carefully about selecting examples that could be easily tweaked by all subject teachers to become a successful addition to their toolkit.

Chapter 1 discusses the process of planning lessons: what pupils will learn; how they will learn it and how you will know if they've learnt it. Here we introduce the two lesson plan formats that we will use throughout the book: the detailed lesson plan for formal observations, and our informal lesson planning template that we use as an everyday tool to ensure we are planning lessons effectively.

Chapters 2–5 each focus on a key aspect of pedagogy for outstanding teaching and learning. They are all structured in the same way:

- **Overview of the chapter topic:** An introduction to the main focus of the chapter.

- **Four strands:** The four main strands of the chapter topic.

- **Tweaking your provision**: Lesson snippets showing the strands in practice. These are the 'tweaks' that you could make to your lessons to improve your provision. Analysis of the tweaks is also provided.

- **Full lesson plans:** The second half of the chapter includes two full lesson plans – a one page plan and a formal lesson plan – both exemplifying the topic and all the strands in action with annotations highlighting top planning techniques.

- **Missed opportunities:** Suggestions for tweaks that could be made to each plan to improve them further, examplifiying how small changes can make a real difference to your practice.

- **Top tweaks checklist:** All of the techniques are summarised at the end of the chapter.

- **Learning leader:** Suggested activities for those who lead professional development in their school or department and want to develop this aspect of pedagogy amongst staff. Activities can be used in departmental development sessions or for staff training in a range of other settings ranging from short after school meetings to INSET days.

- **Links to blogs:** Throughout the chapters are links to key blogs that we have learnt so much from and recommended you read to improve your practice even further.

A summary of the topics covered in each chapter:

Chapter 2 explores the differences between surface and deep Assessment for Learning (AfL). We look at the relationship between pupils and teachers using AfL to help pupils become aware of the progress they are making during lessons and strategies for further improvement to ensure they make excellent progress. We delve into the key aspects of AfL through lesson snippets that show: how to construct and share challenging learning intentions, different ways to model and share high quality exemplars, more sophisticated methods for peer feedback and a range of effective strategies for reviewing learning.

Chapter 3 examines the importance of planning questions into every lesson to stretch all pupils and probe their understanding. We use examples of lesson scenarios to discuss the use of questioning for a range of different purposes: to encourage pupils to think deeply, to check understanding, to support reflection and review progress and to enable pupils to consistently ask effective questions of their peers.

Chapter 4 gives the bigger picture of what stretch and challenge looks like in the classroom. We steer away from seeing challenge as something only for the most able pupils and consider the need for pupils of all abilities to experience enriching and challenging lessons. The lesson examples in this chapter examine challenging every pupil through: the use of different grouping strategies, the provision of choices, developing independence and the role of collaborative learning.

Chapter 5 investigates how teachers can plan lessons to enable their pupils to become more resilient and committed to their learning. We look at the importance of creating an environment where pupils support and challenge each other's learning and have less reliance on the teacher to provide all of the answers. Here, lesson snippets explore dealing with getting stuck, developing growth mindsets, creating a classroom culture of excellence and improving the ability of pupils to listen to and learn from each other.

Chapter 6 examines the role of marking and feedback in helping pupils to make progress. We discuss strategies to manage the marking workload and how to make marking effective, useful and lead to pupils acting on the feedback to improve further. We analyse more blog posts written by our online peers who we highly recommended you track down follow and learn from.

There are also online resources that accompany this book. Log on to www.bloomsbury.com/lesson-planning-tweaks and follow the instructions to download printable lesson plan templates and more.

1 An introduction to lesson planning

Our relationship with the lesson plan has had its highs and lows. When we started out as trainee teachers, with a mammoth nine lessons a week to teach, we spent a ridiculous amount of time planning. We had the luxury of time so thought nothing of spending an hour making matching activity cards or attractive-looking worksheets for our classes – sometimes, we even laminated them! We both have cringeworthy memories of including completely irrelevant activities in our lesson plans so that we were including VAK (Visual, Auditory and Kinaesthetic) learning. Why? We equated the amount of time planning lessons and making resources with being a committed teacher.

One particular memory of lesson planning that we have from our first year – and we are not going to reveal which one of us this particular episode relates to in order to spare our blushes – includes going to a CPD session where the speaker was advocating the importance of visual aids. The next lesson observation featured one of us holding up a banana in class and comparing it with images of bananas on leaflets. It seemed like a good idea at the time; unfortunately, the banana had been in the bottom of the handbag all day making it a very sorry-looking banana by the time period five arrived. Oh, and this was a Year 10 lesson and three quarters of the pupils were male!'

Another inspiring lesson plan involved getting all of the pupils to try and clap in time whilst counting to 20 as one of us shouted out random numbers to put them off! You may be asking what this has to do with learning. Well, not much. However, it did seem like a great activity which showed off the pupils' ability to manage distractions. For anyone who has worked in a school that has had 'Learning to Learn' training in the past decade, activities like these will be all too familiar.

We are sharing these embarrassing moments because we want to make absolutely clear that we are not planning gurus. What we do have though, is a lot of experience in planning really terrible lessons and working out what made them so terrible. Nearly all of our faux pas have happened because of our misguided attempts to do something exciting after attending CPD training or because those higher up had been promoting a particular style of teaching.

Recently, we were having a conversation about when we realised we were going about lesson planning in the wrong way, and we think it was probably when we became Advanced Skills Teachers and had the chance to observe colleagues across schools throughout the year. Having this great opportunity allowed us to see that great lessons had one thing in common: the teachers were clear in what they wanted the pupils to learn and the pupils were clear on how they were going to learn, and the direction in which they were headed to ensure they were going to be successful. That's it. Some lessons were active; some lessons were more passive. Some lessons had group work; some lessons had none. Some lessons involved technology; in some lessons pupils wrote in their exercise books.

Our thinking on lesson planning was clarified when we read an excellent blog by headteacher Stephen Tierney, who blogs as @LeadingLearner (see references for further details). Stephen's experience of observing lessons is that the best lessons are those that focus on the learner rather than the activities. Yet, how quickly do we all fall into the trap of focusing too much of our time on the types of activities we plan rather than spending enough time on constructing challenging learning intentions for our pupils?

When reading this book, think carefully about the learning that is happening in the lessons we describe; the excellent teachers who created the plans have thought carefully about which activities are most useful in developing their pupils' learning. These are also activities which the teachers use all of the time so that their pupils are familiar with the expectations and routines of their teachers' classrooms and not a minute of time is wasted. Our advice when planning is, to focus on structuring a lesson that will enable pupils to have the best chance of learning something challenging, and having a bank of activities which do not require masses of resourcing so can easily be tweaked to suit the needs of your pupils.

Our lesson plans

Throughout this book we will show you examples of lesson plans we or colleagues of ours have written. Each chapter contains two full lesson plans, presented in two different templates:

- **The formal lesson plan**
  We use this format to plan formal observed lessons. It has evolved based upon our own experiences, feedback from colleagues across a range of subjects and levels of experience and the changes to the Ofsted criteria.

- **The one page plan**
  Our simpler and quicker plan, the 'one page plan', is based on the formal lesson plan but is designed to be completed in a few minutes, whilst ensuring all key elements that are needed for a successful lesson are considered.

The pages that follow include photocopiable templates of the two plans (these are also available to download from the online resources) as well as a detailed breakdown of the key elements.

The formal lesson plan

Teacher	Date and period	Subject	Class and ability range	Boy:girl ratio
	Student context:	EAL	SEN	G&T

Learning objective	Differentiated learning outcomes		

Resources needed	Health and safety considerations		

Lesson content			Planned opportunities to check prior knowledge and further pupil progress
The hook			
Tasks			
Reflection			

Differentiation strategies used in the lesson H – Hook T – Tasks R – Reflection	Through task	Through questioning all stages	Through groupings	Through teacher and other adults' support

Literacy/numeracy links

Homework task

© Melanie Aberson & Debbie Light, 2015

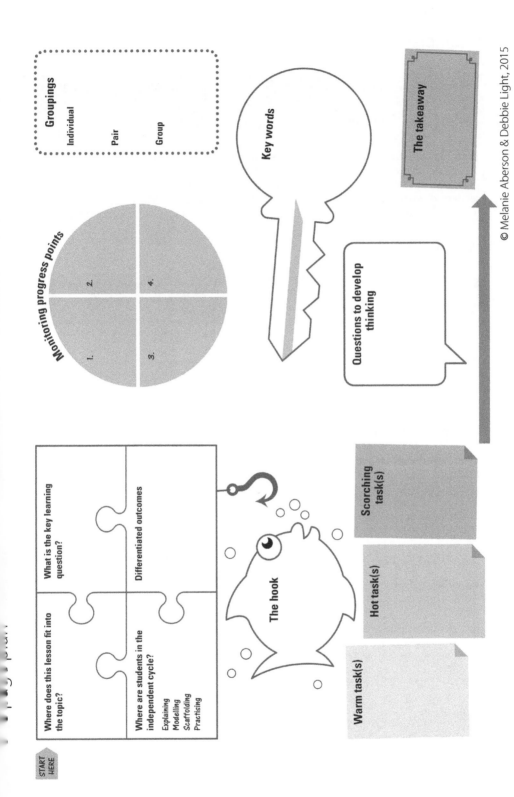

Groupings

Individual

Pair

Group

Key words

The takeaway

Monitoring progress points

1.   2.

3.   4.

Questions to develop thinking

Scorching task(s)

Hot task(s)

Warm task(s)

The hook

Where does this lesson fit into the topic?

What is the key learning question?

Where are students in the independent cycle?

Explaining
Modelling
Scaffolding
Practising

Differentiated outcomes

START HERE

An introduction to lesson planning

A completed formal lesson plan

Teacher Mr Clark	Date and period 25/5/P1	Subject Sociology	Class and ability range Year 10 TMGs C–A*	Boy:girl ratio 3:17
	Student context:	EAL 1	SEN 4	G&T 4

Learning objective	Differentiated learning outcomes
To identify and evaluate the reason that ethnic minorities are over-represented in the crime statistics.	1. Explain why ethnic minorities are over-represented in the crime statistics. 2. Evaluate the reasons for this. 3. Provide a balanced argument for and against and decide which argument is stronger.

Resources needed
PowerPoint, differentiated prompts, handout, sugar paper.

Lesson content	Planned opportunities to check prior knowledge and further pupil progress
The hook – 10mins Before students see title slide and learning objectives, they work in groups to answer questions about the picture on the whiteboard (slide 1). Students discuss in their groups the five Ws and then nominate one person to feedback to the whole group. 5mins discussion and 5mins feedback.	Teacher moves around all students questioning their progress, checking their assumptions about the image and asking them to justify their answers.
Share learning objectives Linking the objectives to assessment objectives and grade boundaries.	
Set homework task Over-representation is discussed using slide 5. *Students given handout.*	Teacher to question higher ability students to draw out reasons for over-representation before they are given handout.
Task – Mini debate Students are given specific roles (differentiated by ability) to take part in mini debates. They will prepare both sides of the argument and a higher ability student will be assigned to each group in order to chair and guide the debate. (*See role card resources and slides 6 and 7.*) 5mins preparing. 5mins debating.	Teacher moves around all students questioning their progress, checking their progress and monitoring use of role cards.
Reflection 5mins feeding back (this will be feedback from the high ability 'chairs' who will have to explain which pair had the stronger argument and justify their decision).	Questioning targeted according to ability.

Breakdown of the formal lesson plan

Top boxes

The top boxes (shaded grey) are the standard administrative points about the class being taught which will be found on most lesson plan pro forma. The 'Differentiated learning outcomes' box is important to ensure that the teacher considers what they expect the pupils (of different ability levels) to achieve.

This section also includes the learning objective for the lesson and the resources you will need.

Lesson content

The lesson content section still contains the constituents of a three-part or episodic lesson, however, the teacher is encouraged to alternate between the 'Task' and 'Reflection' sections to encourage the use of mini plenaries as opposed to one final reflection at the end of the lesson. This ensures that you build in opportunities to monitor how the pupils are responding to the new concept, knowledge or skill being introduced throughout the lesson and allows pupils to consider the progress they are making. Moreover, the main section of the lesson, the 'tasks', are where the majority of the new learning is intended to occur. If a lesson is to be graded outstanding, pupils must experience an element of newness: either new content or new application of previous ideas or skills in order to make rapid and sustained progress.

Note that the 'Planned opportunities to check prior knowledge and further pupil progress' box is intentionally next to the 'Lesson content' box so that, for each activity you consider how the progress made by pupils can be monitored. Some of the questions we most commonly ask colleagues following a lesson observation are: 'What progress have your pupils made?' and 'How do you know?' This box aims to encourage you to consider these vital points at every stage of your planning.

Formal lesson plan continued

Lesson content	Planned opportunities to check prior knowledge and further pupil progress
Task – Written task *(slide 8)* Students write a balanced argument from both perspectives. First they will write from the perspective of a journalist accusing the police of injustice.	Students read partner's argument and respond to or critique the arguments.
Reflection Students swap books and read the argument of their peer.	
Task Students then write a reply from the opposite perspective to their peer. Higher level encouraged to specifically criticise their peer's article. Students pass books on again, read both paragraphs and reflect on where they stand in relation to both arguments.	Teacher to take in written activity to mark and check progress.
Reflection Having reflected on the previous activity, students must line up along a continuum to demonstrate which side of the argument they believe to be stronger. They are encouraged not to become polarised but can be somewhere in the middle. Students will be questioned on their standpoint.	Teacher questions students to demonstrate progress.

Differentiation strategies used in the lesson	Through task	Through questioning all stages	Through groupings	Through teacher and other adults' support
H – Hook T –Tasks R – Reflection	H – Help box at front of class with prompt questions to help guide lower ability. T – Role differentiated by ability. Lower ability will always be paired with higher ability. T – Through outcome in written and extension tasks.	Teacher targets differentiated questions to help students identify next steps and solve problems.	H – mixed ability T – role of 'chair' assigned to high ability students. Pairs are mixed higher with lower abilities.	Teacher supports Grade C students throughout but they are also supported through groupings.

Literacy/numeracy links
Targeted questioning linked with sociological skills.

Homework task
Set at the start of lesson: Using the internet and the library, research the murder of Stephen Lawrence and the Macpherson report. Write a paragraph summarising your findings.

Differentiation

Differentiation is an area that many colleagues have said they find challenging in their planning. The 'Differentiation' section at the bottom of the lesson plan form on page 8 (also shaded grey) was designed to make this easier and more explicit. It allows you to select the differentiation strategies that will be used for each activity in the lesson from four categories:

- **Through task** – strategies may involve having a range of tasks or different resources or worksheets available
- **Through questioning** – reminds you to plan the questions that you (or the pupils) will be asking of different ability groups
- **Through groupings** – prompts you to consider how you are grouping pupils to get the most from each task
- **Through teacher and other adults' support** – allows you to really think carefully about how you and any teaching assistant will spend their time during the lesson. For example, during one lesson you may focus your support more with middle ability pupils to ask them challenging questions and give targeted verbal feedback during an extended task.

Literacy/numeracy links

There is where to identify how pupils' skills in literacy and numeracy are being developed during the lesson. The teaching of literacy and numeracy across the curriculum is a key focus for all schools; accordingly this is explicitly considered in the lesson plan.

Homework task

A vital part of the learning process, the homework box is for you to consider how best to reinforce the learning from the lesson. Homework should challenge pupils to work more independently, but provide differentiated support and resources as appropriate for each class.

A completed one page plan

Where does this lesson fit into the topic?

GCSE Science:
Air quality 11 of 12

What is the key learning question?

What changes can we make to improve air quality?

Where are students in the independent cycle?

Explaining
Modelling
Scaffolding
(Practising)

Differentiated outcomes

1. Identify air quality improvement measures and their effects
2. Give some pros and cons of these measures
3. Evaluate the costs and benefits of a range of air quality measures

The hook

Key word dingbats

Warm task(s)

- Select appropriate success criteria from a list based on the learning objective
- Local air quality improvements and effects poster
- Written reflection task: W

Hot task(s)

- Re-write the success criteria in pupil-friendly language
- National air quality improvements and effects poster
- Written reflection task: H

Scorching task(s)

- Write the success criteria from the learning objective provided
- International air quality improvements and effects poster
- Written reflection task: S

Breakdown of the one page plan

As with the majority of colleagues, the more formal lesson plan is not something we would use day in, day out; it is just for observed lessons or when planning collaboratively with colleagues we are supporting. This 'one page plan' was designed after seeing the 5 minute lesson plan from Ross Morrison McGill (@TeacherToolkit on Twitter, and his blog: teachertoolkit.me.). We thought the informal nature of his plan was a very good idea, however, we needed to make a template that reflected our teaching style, for example by introducing the tasks as warm/hot/scorching and considering the stage of independence that pupils are working at. We recommend you start by filling in the jigsaw section to consider the context of the lesson along with the takeaway, which helps to focus on the most important learning point. It is likely that you will flick between the remaining sections, considering the appropriate groupings, questions and reflections on progress (monitoring progress points) as you design the hook and tasks. You may add to the key words list as you go or jot these all down at the end.

The jigsaw section

This area provides the context for the lesson by identifying where in the topic this lesson fits, the learning objective written in the form of a key learning question and the differentiated learning outcomes. It also allows you to specify where you are in the independent learning cycle by circling the appropriate stage. This ensures you are considering how much support your pupils would be expected to need, and helps an observer understand the level of guidance that is offered.

The hook

The hook immediately engages the class to help them to be ready to learn as soon as they enter the classroom. We use activities that require very little planning and often an element of competition to encourage thinking from the very start of the lesson. Examples of hooks would include: presenting the scrabble letters and their scores and asking pupils to make words relating to the last lesson with the highest possible score, or showing pupils sets of four words, numbers or objects from which they decide on an odd one out and justify their choice.

Tasks

Here the new learning that comprises the main body of the lesson is identified. In order to help plan appropriate differentiation these are allocated one of three possible levels on the plan, which we identify as warm, hot and scorching. We have found that this terminology is easy for pupils to understand and encourages them to challenge themselves. It has been adapted in various ways, for example by describing tasks in terms of different chillies!

One page plan continued

Monitoring progress points

1. T checks each group's work
2. T questions individuals during strategies task
3. Peer assessment of reflection task
4. T takes in reflection task to mark

Groupings

Individual
- Reflection written task

Pair
- Dingbats hook

Group
- Success criteria task in ability groups (of 3/4)
- Summary of strategies task in mixed ability groups

Key words

Catalytic converter
Particulates
Emissions
Pollutant
Efficiency
Wet scrubbers

Questions to develop thinking

Would this be a difficult change to implement? Why?
Why might people not want to do that?
How could people be encouraged to recycle/use public transport?

The takeaway

Write a Tweet summarising how to improve air quality

Monitoring progress points

These are the reflection points in your lesson, or 'mini plenaries' as discussed in the full lesson plan. They enable you to monitor progress and allow the pupils to reflect on and demonstrate the learning they have achieved.

Groupings

An important consideration that it can be very easy to forget is the groupings. This space on the plan is to remind you that groupings need to be planned carefully. There is space to identify which tasks will be completed individually, in a pair or in a larger group as well as what the composition of these groups will be, for example talk pairs, ability groups or practical mixed ability groups.

Key words

Some subjects require a vast amount of terminology to be used appropriately, so by identifying the key words for each lesson you can ensure that pupils are introduced to appropriate terminology as required without being overloaded.

Questions to develop thinking

We have highlighted the importance of questioning in this book by dedicating a whole chapter to it. Having this box on the plan ensures we explicitly plan particular questions for each lesson.

If nothing else, plan the questions you will ask. Some teachers become so skilled at questioning that it appears effortless and unplanned. This has, however, developed into mastery over years of practice, and time invested in planning quality questions is time well spent.

The takeaway

We have found it useful to consider the most important point from the lesson that the teacher would want the pupils to take away and remember. We often ask our pupils to reflect on their learning towards the end of a lesson and decide themselves what they consider the takeaway to be. This can be very enlightening as pupils sometimes come up with a completely different key learning point than expected, but it is very useful feedback for the teacher when planning the subsequent lessons!

Planning a lesson

Whichever plan we are using, the process is the same. We start by thinking about 'the takeaway', the key learning point that you want pupils to leave knowing or being able to do. (The equivalent on the formal lesson plan is the final reflection activity). This helps us to construct or adapt (if using an existing scheme of work) an appropriate learning objective or key learning question. This is an important point to start with, as sometimes we can be so busy thinking about trying out the fantastic activity that we found on Twitter, that we forget the most important aspect of the lesson: What do I want my pupils to learn?

The differentiated learning outcomes may exist in a scheme of work but we should always consider the individual pupils in our class. What is the most challenging outcome that I would really push the most able pupils to achieve on a good day? That will be my 'scorching' or highest level outcome. How can I tweak this to still meet the learning objective but to be more suitable for a middle or lower level pupil to aim for?

Next, we take a moment to reflect on where this lesson falls in the topic and thus how much support we intend to provide. If we are starting a topic, do we need to spend a significant proportion of time explaining a new concept or technique? If we are a little further along, how will we model the process? Will we do this during the lesson or use a video to demonstrate it? Alternatively, is there a pupil who is more accomplished in this particular topic and could explain what they would do next?

If we are beyond this (although it may still be useful to revisit explaining and modelling), how will we provide scaffolding for our pupils to leave them confident to get on without our guidance? Finally, how can the pupils practise the new learning to ensure they have 'practised enough to better understand what they are doing?' (Lemov et. al., 2012).

The hooks enable us to settle our class to be ready to learn whilst giving us a chance to take the register and catch up with the pupil who missed their detention. It is best to try out two or three different hooks at a time with a class to get them into a routine and to make planning simpler. These activities are designed to provide a challenge whilst requiring minimal preparation and teacher input to run, so we might use Scrabble, Odd one out and Would you rather? with a Key Stage 4 class and Dingbats, Taboo and What happened next? with a Key Stage 3 class.

The tasks are the main activities that enable pupils to meet the learning objective. The tasks may be differentiated themselves, or through the amount of support that pupils can use to complete them. As we plan these we will also consider the grouping that would be most effective to ensure all pupils are appropriately challenged or have the opportunity to experience a range of opinions and experiences during discussion.

After considering each task and referring back to the desired outcomes, we plan how pupils will reflect on their learning and their progress against the outcomes or success criteria during or after the planned tasks.

2 Assessment for Learning

(Not to be confused with getting the pupils to mark their own books so you don't have to ...)

Of all the initiatives that have been and gone, Assessment for Learning (AfL) has stayed at the forefront of what is considered excellent practice. AfL was introduced to schools at the beginning of the new millennium with the seminal work, *Inside the black box* (Black and Wiliam, 1998), written by leading academics at King's College, London. Their findings were that the more pupils were able to understand how they were being assessed and how to use feedback from their teachers in their next assessment, the more pupils' attainment increased. The DfE (or DfES as it was then) quickly took on these ideas and made them integral to judging the quality of learning and teaching. Over ten years on, AfL remains firmly on the agenda and the best teachers make AfL the fabric of the lesson, rather than a clunky bolt-on.

What does this mean in practice? First of all, pupils will need a range of opportunities during a lesson to stop and reflect on where they are at, where they need to get to and how they are going to get there. Teachers need to engage their pupils in oral and written feedback to let them know how they can move to the next level in their learning. Furthermore, this engagement between pupils and teachers is made much easier if there is a shared language of assessment in the classroom, making the assessment criteria as transparent as possible and communicated using language that pupils are able to understand.

Constructing and sharing challenging learning intentions

Constructing a challenging learning intention should be one of the first things you think about when planning a lesson. Teachers frame their learning intentions in different ways; some phrase them as learning objectives, some use WALT (we are learning to) and others use a key learning question. Regardless of what you use, the learning intention needs to focus on what you want the pupils to learn in that lesson. This is not to be confused with what the pupils will be doing in the lesson – the learning outcomes. Think carefully about the pupils you have in your classes. Don't limit their learning by constructing an easily achievable learning intention. Rather, choose a challenging one and then scaffold your lesson appropriately to ensure all pupils have a chance to show you what they have learnt.

Lesson snippet 1

Lesson context: Year 8 Science, mixed ability class

The teacher shares the learning outcomes with the pupils. Pupils discuss in pairs which outcomes they think are more challenging and rank them. Then pupils write down what they think might be the learning objective based on the learning outcomes.

Learning objective: To understand how to carry out a successful electromagnetism investigation.

Learning outcomes:

Warm – To make an electromagnet and collect some results for your investigation.

Hot – To plot a graph and explain what the results show.

Scorching – To analyse the results and evaluate the method used.

The tweak

Share the learning objective and structure the outcomes to encourage pupils to challenge themselves.

Beginning with the learning outcomes rather than the objective is a successful strategy you could use to help pupils think about what they know, what they want to achieve and how they will apply their new learning. To begin, pupils are engaging in good discussion by having to think about which outcomes are more challenging; they will be drawing on prior knowledge to make the correct choices as well as beginning to see the differences in complexity. This idea is then extended further by getting the pupils to consider what the learning objective might be – a difficult task that will need the pupils to look at all of the outcomes before piecing them together to see the bigger learning picture. By introducing this task early on in the lesson, the pupils then have a very clear idea about what they are doing, why they are doing it and what their personal challenge is for the lesson.

How I've tried to share learning intentions better
Harry Fletcher-Wood (improvingteaching.co.uk) 6 October 2013.

Lesson snippet 2

Lesson context: Year 11 GCSE PE theory, mixed ability class

Pupils are given a key word literacy mat, an A4-sized learning resource with ten subject-specific words based on the topic of creating training programmes for athletes. The teacher shares the learning objective in the format of a key learning question: What would be a successful training programme for an athlete looking to improve their cardiovascular function? The first learning outcome is shared with pupils: to describe three elements of an appropriate training programme using at least four of the key words on the literacy mat. This outcome is labelled 'multistructural' from SOLO taxonomy. Using the key words on the literacy mats, pupils are instructed to create either a 'relational' outcome or an 'extended abstract' outcome to support them in answering their key learning question. Pupils pin up their outcomes on the board and categorise them as either 'relational' or 'extended abstract'. The teacher uses these outcomes throughout the lesson as a prompt for further discussion on developing more sophisticated responses since most pupils were only able to describe on their first attempt in a previous lesson.

The tweak

Use SOLO (structure of observed learning outcomes) taxonomy to structure learning outcomes.

In this example, the teacher uses SOLO taxonomy to structure their learning outcomes. The pupils are familiar with the different concepts of 'multistructural' (having several pieces of knowledge), 'relational' (being able to make connection between the different pieces of knowledge) and 'extended abstract' (being able to take the knowledge learnt and apply it to a new context or scenario). Some teachers are put off using SOLO taxonomy because of the slightly odd labelling of outcomes; however, even if you don't use the labels, this taxonomy works very well because the outcomes are based on a solid foundation of knowledge that then appropriately builds to more abstract and challenging thinking. Once pupils begin to see that they can build upon their knowledge step by step, they will be able to work out quickly what they can and cannot do. This taxonomy aligns itself very well with many exam board marking criteria which often move from 'describe' to 'explain' to 'analyse' to 'evaluate', mirroring the multistructural, relational and extended abstract learning outcomes. Finally, SOLO taxonomy does not encourage the teacher to rush through the different outcomes; much work needs to be done at the multistructural level so that the pupils have enough of a knowledge base to be able to apply it in a more abstract way later in the lesson or topic.

Lesson snippet 3

Lesson context: Year 7 English, high ability class

Pupils are shown an image of several jigsaw pieces, each one filled with different learning objectives from a series of lessons on a particular topic. The teacher indicates which jigsaw puzzle pieces are left to complete in this topic. There are four jigsaw pieces left with the remaining objectives. Pupils discuss in their table groups which piece they think they will be focusing on in today's lesson to help them progress with their key learning question for their study of Michael Morpurgo's novel *Private Peaceful*: How does Michael Morpurgo's writing style generate different responses from readers? The four jigsaw pieces are displayed in different corners of the room; a spokesperson from each group is asked to stand by the jigsaw piece they believe is most appropriate that they study this lesson. Then pupils are asked to write underneath the jigsaw piece a learning outcome they would expect to achieve if they focused on this learning objective in the lesson.

The tweak

Give pupils a clear visual for the topic's learning map to help them connect their learning from different lessons.

This is another effective example of how to get pupils thinking more deeply about what they are going to learn during a lesson. All of the learning objectives will be covered during the topic, but the pupils have to consider the sequence of the learning objectives. Giving pupils discussion time before standing next to the jigsaw piece they think is the most relevant for this lesson is a good way for pupils to consider all of the options. Having the pupils move to different corners of the room is an easy way for the teacher to identify any patterns in the way pupils have interpreted the task. The follow-up task of pupils producing an appropriate outcome helps the pupils to play an active role in deciding what they think they need to work on to improve their knowledge and understanding.

'New adventures' in SOLO, flipped learning and better learning intentions
Damian Benney (mrbenney.wordpress.com) 22 March 2014.

Expectations
Zoë Elder (marginallearninggains.com) 11 November 2012.

Modelling and sharing high-quality exemplars

Making explicit to pupils how to tackle something new is one of the most vital aspects of lesson planning. There are different ways you can model a new idea or concept to pupils but the teacher needs to have a thorough understanding of what is being taught so that this information can be given to pupils in an accessible way. The better the modelling, the more likely it is that pupils will understand what they are being taught. Linked to this, if pupils have a clear picture in their head of the completed outcome, this will give them something concrete to aim for during their learning. It is time well spent either creating your own high-quality exemplars, finding examples from exam boards or putting together a bank of excellent work from your previous pupils.

Lesson snippet 1

Lesson context: Year 10 Food technology, mixed ability class
The teacher has prepared and laid out a sheet with a QR code on it on every surface. Pupils are put into pairs and given an iPad to scan the QR code, which takes them to a demonstration of different knife skills. Pupils then practise their version of the demonstration. After practising, the teacher selects two able pupils to share their demonstration with the rest of the class. Pupils then critique the two demonstrations, highlighting where their peers have evidenced particular skills.

The tweak

Use new technology to give pupils access to quality exemplars.

The teacher has found a good quality resource which the pupils can use to support them making progress with the knife skills. Pupils are able to judge their own level of skill against the demonstration. In this case, having the QR code with the link to the demonstration is more effective than just watching the teacher model the process because it allows the pupils to pause their work and go back to the video when they get stuck. The task they are doing is fairly complicated, so having the video as and when they need it means they are more likely to make progress with their task than having to remember what the teacher did earlier in the lesson. The next task involving the two pupils showing the rest of the class what they have learnt is an effective way for the class to see high quality examples of knife skills. Choosing two pupils, rather than just one, allows the pupils to use more sophisticated thinking by making subtle comparisons. QR codes are an easy way to give pupils a lot of information in a condensed format. There are several free apps and websites you can download to create QR codes. Using QR codes is a good example of how new technology can enhance learning rather than just using technology in a gimmicky way.

Lesson snippet 2

Lesson context: Year 12 Media arts, mixed ability class

Pupils are set the task of beginning to write evaluations of adverts they have produced. The teacher shares on the board the first draft of an exemplar evaluation and tells pupils that this evaluation would receive a low grade because several aspects of the mark scheme have not been addressed. Pupils are divided into groups of three and each group is given an aspect of the mark scheme to focus on. The pupils begin discussing what might be missing from the evaluation. Once the groups have decided on the changes they would make, one member of the group goes up to the board and makes their changes so that all of the pupils can see the improved draft. Once all of the groups have made their changes, the teacher then makes changes, developing further the new suggestions made by the pupils. Pupils examine the complete mark scheme and check that the improved draft has now met all of the aspects.

The tweak

Introduce good pieces of work that can be improved as a discussion stimulus.

The task of improving an existing example piece of work encourages pupils to understand what a quality piece of work looks like. Sharing a basic evaluation before getting the pupils to write one from scratch is an effective way to support pupils in knowing how to start. Often when pupils are asked to improve a piece of work or look at an exemplar answer, they are given the full mark scheme. This can be daunting, regardless of their age, because there is so much to look for. By separating the mark scheme into sections for each group to focus on, the task immediately becomes more manageable. Once the pupils have made their suggestions to improve the draft evaluation, it is easy for them to see what they need to aim for when writing their own version. The teacher then critiquing the pupils' suggestions is another strategy that pushes the pupils to produce a polished piece of work. Finishing the task with the pupils going back to the mark scheme to check all aspects have been covered means pupils will now have a good working knowledge of what was previously an inaccessible mark scheme.

Pedagogy postcard #3: Live exemplars; iPads and visualisers
Tom Sherrington (headguruteacher.com) 23 March 2014.

Shared writing: Modelling mastery
Alex Quigley (huntingenglish.com) 19 March 2013.

Lesson snippet 3

Lesson context: Year 9 Maths, low ability class

Pupils are given a number of shapes that need to be transformed by rotation and reflection. Pupils watch the teacher draw the transformed shapes on the interactive whiteboard. After modelling the process, the teacher shows three examples of different shapes that have been rotated, one of which has been rotated inaccurately. Pupils are asked to draw on their mini whiteboards the accurate rotation at the same time as the teacher; however the teacher's interactive whiteboard is blanked out so the pupils cannot see the accurate rotation. Pupils then display their mini whiteboards all together and the teacher reveals her rotated shape. Pupils then take back their mini whiteboard; if they did not get the rotation correct, these examples will be used as a basis for class discussion about why they think these errors have occurred.

The tweak

Use mini whiteboards to carry out a quick check to see if pupils have understood what the teacher has modelled.

Teachers modelling elements of their subject to pupils acts as a powerful tool for pupils to see clearly how to do something. This kind of modelling is often undervalued by many teachers and dismissed as 'chalk and talk': nothing could be further from the truth! If teachers do not spend enough time carefully and concisely explaining new information to pupils, then pupils will have a shaky foundation when it comes to applying for themselves what they have learnt from their teacher's explanation. Pupils also appreciate teachers who complete tasks at the same time as them; they secretly hope you will go wrong at some point! There is also an element of competition by having a timed challenge. Not revealing what you have done until the pupils have finished and ready to display their attempt adds an extra element to the task. In the example above, when all of the pupils reveal their whiteboards together, the teacher will instantly be able to identify which pupils have made a mistake and can clear up any misconception, whilst also acknowledging those pupils who have understood the new learning and applied it accurately to complete the task. Pupils who have been successful can continue the lesson by stretching themselves with a more complex task, and those that need extra support can receive it from the teacher, who can model the process once more for a smaller group of pupils.

Teaching sequence for developing independence Stage 2: Model
David Didau (learningspy.co.uk) 30 June 2013.

Peer feedback

Getting pupils to give and receive useful feedback is notoriously difficult. For most pupils, talking about their peers' work can be awkward because they think highlighting the negative points in other pupils' work can be perceived as impolite. This barrier can be overcome by setting up clear protocols for discussing pupils' work and giving pupils the language to critique rather than criticise. Insist on pupils using the language that you have taught them; by doing this, the experience of peer feedback becomes normalised.

Lesson snippet 1

Lesson context: Year 9 Geography, middle ability class

In a previous lesson, pupils have written their analysis of the pros and cons of globalisation. In this follow-up lesson, pupils get into groups of three to feedback on each other's work. Each one in the group is labelled A B C so that they can offer ABC feedback: **A**dd an idea that is missing, **B**uild on a point that is too general, **C**hallenge an idea or correct an inaccuracy. Each pupil looks at two analyses, focusing on their A, B or C aspect of feedback. The pupils then have their analysis passed back to them. The teacher gives them time to look at the changes the pupils have made to their work. The teacher then asks the pupils: based on the feedback you have received today, what are your next steps before you hand in your second draft?

The tweak

Use ABC feedback featured in the blogs of Alex Quigley (@HuntingEnglish).

Using the ABC peer feedback model is a much more useful and advanced way of pupils giving feedback to each other as opposed to the more traditional EBI (Even Better If) model. The problem that can arise with using EBI at the end of a piece of work is that pupils might either offer a simplistic comment such as 'write more', or they may make an insightful point to which the other pupil is unsure how to respond. We've all heard pupils who say: 'But if I knew how to do it, I'd have done it already!' The beauty of ABC peer feedback is pupils are not suggesting changes but are making the changes themselves so pupils receiving the feedback can clearly see what they could have done. The teacher has built in time for the pupils to reflect on the quality of the peer feedback given, which encourages pupils to think about what is useful feedback and the next steps they will take to improve their analysis.

'Disciplined discussion' – As easy as ABC
Alex Quigley (huntingenglish.com) 26 December 2013.

Lesson snippet 2

Lesson context: Year 8 Music, mixed ability class

In this lesson, pupils are working on their compositions based on popular music they have been studying. Each pupil is given generic criteria for an excellent composition. The teacher poses the question: 'How can we use these generic criteria and turn them into specific criteria based on popular music we have studied?' 'What are we listening out for that indicates qualities of a popular music song?' The teacher leads a whole class discussion on the specifics of their composition task. She displays on the interactive whiteboard the generic criteria with another column ready to be filled with the specific criteria. Each pupil has their composition open on the computer ready to listen to. The pupils begin a peer critique by making their way clockwise around the computers; next to each computer is a mini whiteboard where the listener writes down which aspect of the criteria they think is the least developed. Once the task is complete, the teacher asks the pupils to see if there are any patterns in the feedback they have received. Once the pupils have read their feedback, they wipe the mini whiteboard clean and write a message to their teacher about what they are developing during the second half of the lesson. Pupils who are unsure and would like some guidance draw a star on their mini whiteboard to get the teacher's attention.

The tweak

Create a culture of critique by making the process highly visible.

There is a culture of critique in the class, with well-established routines of leaving your work open, moving around the classroom and writing your feedback on the mini whiteboard. Making sure the Year 8 pupils really understand the criteria is essential if the peer feedback is to be a success. Translating it from generic to specific helps pupils to listen out for the good aspects of the composition and give useful feedback. After receiving feedback from each other, the pupils then have to distil it and decide on their own priorities. By writing this on the mini whiteboard, it is easy for the teacher to read it without disturbing the pupils, who will be plugged into the headphones. Pupils sometimes get quite irritated if they are working hard on a piece of work and are interrupted by the teacher peering over their shoulder about to ask how they are getting on. Those that have drawn a star will get the extra dialogue they need with the teacher to progress with the task.

Creating a culture of critique
David Fawcett (reflectionsofmyteaching.blogspot.co.uk) 6 April 2013.

Lesson snippet 3

Lesson context: Year 11 Religious education, mixed ability class

Pupils are preparing for a debate on the topic of evil and suffering. Pupils are in groups of four and each group has been given a different topic to prepare. Pupils are halfway through their time allocation for individually preparing their arguments, and the teacher asks them to pause and verbally share their ideas so far with the rest of their group. Within the group, pupils are paired up and each pair in the group is given a laminated sentence starter mat with examples that might add sophistication to their arguments. Pupils make notes on what they have heard and use the sentence starter mat to develop their partner's arguments. The pupils then return to their own arguments and redraft based on their partner's suggestions. Once all of the pupils in the group have had the chance for feedback, they then rank which arguments are strongest and work together to create their group's argument based on their topic.

The tweak

Use verbal feedback immediately by including time for redrafting.

When giving peer feedback, it is not always necessary to have a detailed mark scheme to judge a pupil's work against. If a pupil's work is being developed over a series of lessons – in this case the pupils had three lessons to prepare for their formal debate – then it may be more useful to focus on one particular aspect and provide some examples to include. Getting pupils using appropriate academic language can be a challenge in subjects across the curriculum: having sentence openers with formal language allows the pupils to offer feedback to improve this area of their arguments. In addition, the teacher's timing for when to build in peer feedback is crucial. The teacher gives the pupils ten minutes to draft their arguments before they have to share anything; this is followed by another ten minutes for listening and suggestions and then another ten minutes to redraft their initial arguments. This task is then extended further by having the pupils rank all of their arguments in order of which ones they think will have the most impact on the opposition. Working in this way means the pupils are constantly working towards excellence, considering possibilities, engaging in genuine dialogue and redrafting their work until it is of the highest quality.

A second bite at the cherry: thoughts on redrafting writing
Andy Tharby (reflectingenglish.wordpress.com) 18 April 2014.

Lessons from berger: Austin's butterfly and not accepting mediocrity
Tom Sherrington (headguruteacher.com) 5 November 2013.

Reviewing learning

How many of us are guilty of not reviewing pupils' learning because we've run out of time? How many of us are guilty of over-reviewing pupils' learning because it makes us think that our pupils must be learning something? How many of us are guilty of reviewing learning in a shallow way and mistaking pupils' performance in a lesson for embedded learning? Reviewing learning is a tricky thing to get right when planning a lesson. The most important questions to consider are how difficult is the learning in this lesson and what is the crucial 'takeaway' I need pupils to remember before I introduce another new element? These questions should inform your decision about when you review the learning, the format it takes and how often it happens.

Lesson snippet 1

Lesson context: Year 7 Computing, mixed ability class
Pupils are working on a talent show project. They have been producing an Excel spreadsheet to add up the judges' scores and it is the last ten minutes of the lesson. Pupils have personalised A6-sized sheets on their desks called 'exit tickets' which have two questions for them to answer: 'What is my takeaway for today?' and 'What do I need help with to challenge myself?' The teacher reminds them that they need to complete their exit tickets in the next five minutes.

The tweak

Make pupils' reflections easy to access by using exit tickets.

The class in the example above are showing a high level of independence for a Year 7 class. The teacher needs to collect information on how a very mixed ability class are getting on and has spent much of the lesson having one-to-one conversations with targeted pupils about their progress. The exit card strategy will enable the teacher to make tweaks to his planning for the next lesson in a week's time to ensure there is an appropriate level of challenge for all pupils. The 'takeaway' is well understood by the pupils as being the most important thing they have learnt from today's lesson and gives the teacher a very good picture of where each pupil is as they leave. The second question is for pupils to identify the area they think they need help with but includes the phrase 'to challenge myself' to ensure pupils realise that asking for help is important in assisting them to make even greater progress. This is a very useful strategy for subjects that have a large number of classes who teachers see less frequently, when it can be difficult to keep track of every pupil.

Lesson snippet 2

Lesson context: Year 10 Art and design, mixed ability class

Pupils are in the early stages of creating a painting with the theme 'order and disorder'. The teacher has left the pupils to get stuck into their painting and there is a countdown timer on the board. The teacher explained to the pupils before they started painting that after 15 minutes she would put a timer on the board for five minutes to represent their 'reflection window'. The pupils have been given a laminated card with *three questions* to help them think about their progress so far. These are: 1. Which success criteria do you think this piece of work meets? 2. What ideas could you take from this piece to use in your work? 3. What would you do next with this piece of work? The laminate also lists three things to look for in pieces that other pupils have produced. Pupils use drywipe pens to fill in their card during this reflection window.

The tweak

Allocate a window of time for pupil reflection to accommodate different speeds of learning.

So often in lessons, particularly when being observed, we panic that we must regularly drop everything to show the progress that our pupils have made. Whilst it is important for pupils to take time to reflect on where they are and where they need to go next, it often ends up being a case of, 'OK stop the learning now to think about the learning!' Pupils who are in mid flow might be irritated by having to stop at that precise point to demonstrate their progress. By agreeing at the start of a task that there will be a time period for reflection and giving pupils the choice of when this is most appropriate for them, you avoid interrupting their progress and give more control to your pupils.

'Outstanding'... who me? Never!
Sarah Findlater (msfindlater.blogspot.co.uk) 27 January 2013.

Unlocking the power of progress
Sarah Findlater (msfindlater.blogspot.co.uk) 22 February 2013.

Lesson snippet 3

Lesson context: Year 13 Spanish, mixed ability class

The class are learning about the issues of racism and the teacher is trying to develop their listening skills. Pupils have listened to a radio podcast about racism in football and have written a summary of the podcast in Spanish. This is a class of just seven pupils, so each reads out a short section of their summary and the rest of the class listen. Two pupils are selected to make a comment or ask a question about what each pupil reads out. The teacher has her mobile phone on the desk and records each pupil as they read as well as the questions or comments and responses.

The tweak

Use technology to record pupils to support them in reviewing their learning.

With smaller classes it can be assumed that it is much easier for the teacher to have a good picture of the progress made by every pupil. What is more difficult, however, is to monitor skills such as speaking and listening which are vital for the study of languages. Asking pupils to read out their work in this way has many benefits: they have an immediate audience, so are more likely to put in their best effort; they are practising their speaking skills and their peers are practising their listening skills by having to ask questions in response; the teacher can focus on the content during the lesson but listen back to the recording (or even play it back to pupils in the next lesson) to give feedback on pronunciation, grammar and intonation.

Progress in my classroom with Socrative
Mark Anderson (ictevangelist.com) 2 April 2013.

Is there a place for multiple-choice in English? Part I
Phil Stock (joeybagstock.wordpress.com) 20 November 2013.

Annotated History lesson plan

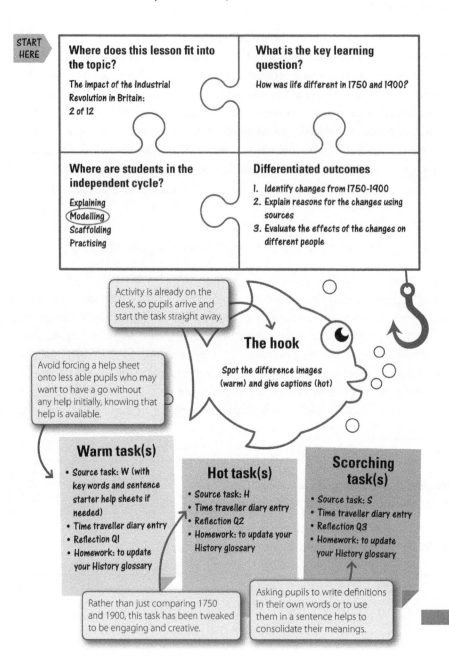

START HERE

Where does this lesson fit into the topic?

The impact of the Industrial Revolution in Britain:
2 of 12

What is the key learning question?

How was life different in 1750 and 1900?

Where are students in the independent cycle?

Explaining
Modelling
Scaffolding
Practising

Differentiated outcomes

1. Identify changes from 1750-1900
2. Explain reasons for the changes using sources
3. Evaluate the effects of the changes on different people

Activity is already on the desk, so pupils arrive and start the task straight away.

The hook

Spot the difference images (warm) and give captions (hot)

Avoid forcing a help sheet onto less able pupils who may want to have a go without any help initially, knowing that help is available.

Warm task(s)

- Source task: W (with key words and sentence starter help sheets if needed)
- Time traveller diary entry
- Reflection Q1
- Homework: to update your History glossary

Hot task(s)

- Source task: H
- Time traveller diary entry
- Reflection Q2
- Homework: to update your History glossary

Scorching task(s)

- Source task: S
- Time traveller diary entry
- Reflection Q3
- Homework: to update your History glossary

Rather than just comparing 1750 and 1900, this task has been tweaked to be engaging and creative.

Asking pupils to write definitions in their own words or to use them in a sentence helps to consolidate their meanings.

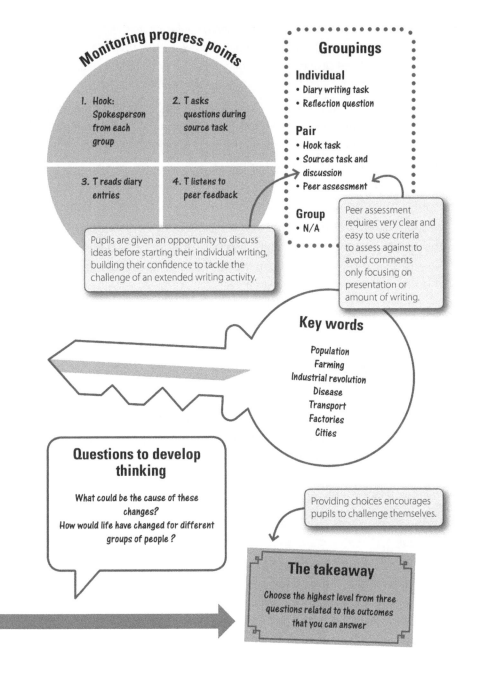

Monitoring progress points

1. Hook: Spokesperson from each group

2. T asks questions during source task

3. T reads diary entries

4. T listens to peer feedback

Groupings

Individual
- Diary writing task
- Reflection question

Pair
- Hook task
- Sources task and discussion
- Peer assessment

Group
- N/A

Pupils are given an opportunity to discuss ideas before starting their individual writing, building their confidence to tackle the challenge of an extended writing activity.

Peer assessment requires very clear and easy to use criteria to assess against to avoid comments only focusing on presentation or amount of writing.

Key words

Population
Farming
Industrial revolution
Disease
Transport
Factories
Cities

Questions to develop thinking

What could be the cause of these changes?
How would life have changed for different groups of people ?

Providing choices encourages pupils to challenge themselves.

The takeaway

Choose the highest level from three questions related to the outcomes that you can answer

AfL provision in History lesson plan

- The lesson plan begins with the teacher clearly explaining to the pupils the learning objective and the differentiated learning outcomes. Setting up the lesson in this way means the pupils are clear from the beginning about what they are learning and what they will have to do during the lesson to achieve the different levels.

- The time traveller diary entry is an engaging and creative task which is enjoyable for the pupils. This individual task is a good opportunity for the teacher to monitor the progress the pupils are making against the learning objective and intervene where necessary with pupils who are struggling.

- Pupils will peer assess each other's work using the success criteria. Criteria are matched to different levels of outcome for the lesson. Pupils use the feedback from their peer to adapt their work next time around in order to move up the levels.

- The three questions at the end of the lesson will identify to the teacher and pupils whether they are able to respond to the learning objective set at the beginning of the lesson. Sharing aloud three of the responses will allow other pupils to hear responses which are different to theirs, thus developing their understanding of the topic.

Missed opportunities and tweaks

Missed opportunity

The teacher needs to wait until the end of the individual writing task (15 minutes) to see whether the pupils have understood the learning objective. There are no other points in the lesson where the teacher has planned opportunities for pupils to reflect on what progress they are making in meeting the learning objective and what support (if any) they will need in getting there.

The tweak

A more effective use of time would be if you ask pupils to take a pit stop as they approach the halfway point of a longer written task. The pupils could read what they have written so far to their partner. Using the criteria, pupils could offer one thing their peer needs to do in the second half of the writing task. This means your pupils have time to make changes which will lead to more progress being made during the lesson, rather than waiting to the end of the task to discover whether they have missed out an important part of the criteria.

Missed opportunity

The success criteria that the teacher gives to the pupils will only be distributed at the end of the writing task for the peer assessment activity. Effectively, this means that pupils are engaging in a writing task – the main opportunity for establishing what progress is being made by pupils – without having a clear idea of what criteria they will be assessed against.

The tweak

Before beginning with the writing task, you should lead the class in co-constructing the success criteria. Have the subject success descriptors out and ask pupils to translate these general descriptors into specific criteria for this time traveller writing task. These criteria can then be referred to during the writing task.

In summary...

The lesson needs to be well designed to help the pupils know: what they need to learn, what skills they will use during the lesson and whether there is evidence that they have met the learning objective. Success criteria should be shared when starting a task and, ideally, constructed with input from the pupils so they can cement their understanding of the points they are trying to achieve.

For you to be able to effectively intervene when pupils are struggling or coasting, it is vital that you plan regular opportunities to reflect throughout the lesson. The mini plenary doesn't need to be a complicated activity that interrupts the learning, see the 'Reviewing learning' lesson snippets and blog suggestions for further ideas (page 29).

Annotated Media arts lesson plan

Teacher	Date and period	Subject	Class and ability range	Boy:girl ratio
Mrs Diamond	12/03/P2	Media arts	Year 11 Mixed	9:13
Student context:		**EAL** 3	**SEN** 2 MLD; 3 BESD	**G&T** 0

Learning objective	Differentiated learning outcomes
To understand how to use specific conventions of a music video in our own work.	1. Identify a range of visual and audio conventions in a music video and apply some of these to their own work. 2. Select the most appropriate conventions of a music video to use that match the genre of their chosen music video to create an effect on the target audience. 3. Explore the effect of specific music video conventions on different target audiences and use some of these conventions in an original and innovative way to create an effect on their own target audience.

> Before sharing the learning objective, the teacher uses an activity to immediately engage pupils and prepare them for the direction of the lesson, whilst checking their prior learning.

Resources needed
Rihanna music video, One Direction music video, music video conventions grids, computers, video making software.

Lesson content	Planned opportunities to check prior knowledge and further pupil progress
Starter activity Pupils asked to discuss in their groups what is the most obvious convention in a music video from different genres: R & B; pop; rock; dance.	Teacher can check pupils' prior knowledge and follow up accordingly based on pupil responses to starter activity.
Teacher takes feedback from each group, who are given one genre to feed back on. Teacher asks specific pupils to add to the feedback from each group and challenges them to think why this convention is appropriate for the particular genre.	> By asking different groups to feed back on different genres, the feedback does not become repetitive. The teacher ensures pupils remain focused by asking them to add comments on other groups' feedback.
Teacher introduces learning objective and outcomes to pupils, explaining the requirements for each grade. This will focus particularly on the differences between the requirements for a grade D and a grade C as this is appropriate for this class.	
New learning activities Pupils view the Rihanna and One Direction music videos. Using their conventions grid, pupils identify when the conventions are used and the effect on the target audience.	Pupils' completed conventions grids are monitored by the teacher.
Teacher targets certain pupils to share their thoughts on what they consider to be the most effective convention for each music video. Other pupils are asked to consider which music video they think is the most original for its genre.	

Lesson content	Planned opportunities to check prior knowledge and further pupil progress
Pupils return to their music videos. In this lesson, all are expected to complete the first 15 seconds of the video and some are expected to include titles as well.	Teacher monitors pupils' work on the computers, questioning pupils further to prompt or develop their ideas.
Reflection activities Mini plenary after viewing: pupils share their grids with the other pupils in their group to identify ideas to improve their own work.	
Final plenary: another pupil working in the same genre views their partner's music video so far and offers suggestions on how to improve it. These suggestions are recorded in their music video production log as targets for the next lesson.	Pupils' logs are monitored throughout the production schedule.

Differentiation strategies used in the lesson	Through task	Through questioning all stages	Through groupings	Through teacher and other adults' support
S – Starter NL – New learning activity R – Reflection activity T - Throughout	S – Each group is given a different genre to consider, which provide different levels of challenge in this task. NL – Some of the pupils are expected to add titles to their 15 seconds of video.	S – Teacher chooses weaker pupils to share ideas from the group to support their participation in the lesson. NL – Teacher chooses most able to share convention grid comparisons.	S – Mixed ability groupings. NL – Individual work. R – Ability pairs.	Teacher supports the three E grade pupils at the beginning of the practical work and then moves to two A grade pupils to help develop original ideas with them.

Literacy/numeracy links
- Subject-specific vocabulary written on board based on music video conventions.
- Pupils need to consider the timings of transitions in their music videos.

Homework task
- To write in their logs about their improvements in using the software as well as anything they are finding difficult.

Assessment for Learning

37

AfL provision in Media arts lesson plan

- The group starter activity allows the pupils to use their discussion skills and work with other pupils to revise and recap on prior learning.

- There is time for the teacher to clearly explain what is required for a D, C, B, A or A*. She plans to particularly highlight the difference between a D and a C as most of the class seem to have this target minimum grade (TMG).

- The conventions grid resource is an effective way of supporting pupils to learn the conventions as well as monitoring whether all pupils understand them, based on how much of the grid is completed.

- When pupils share their grids with their group, this is an opportunity for pupils to compare their ideas with others. Some pupils can make changes to their grids afterwards, showing the progress they are making after moving from an individual to a group activity.

- When pupils receive feedback from their peer, there are five minutes allocated in the plan for this conversation, which is sufficient for pupils to listen and respond to their peer's ideas.

- The use of the music video production logs is an effective way for pupils and teacher to monitor the learning during production time. It helps pupils to see the bigger picture by recording all of their issues and feedback in one place.

Missed opportunities and tweaks

Missed opportunity

The teacher decided to have eight groups for the starter activity. There were two groups for each musical genre. There is no opportunity in the plan for these two groups to come together and discuss their ideas. This may be a moment when pupils can develop their knowledge further.

The tweak

If you choose to set up an activity where there is more than one pair or group focusing on the same area, plan time for them to join up and compare their ideas using a specific criterion to judge the quality of their ideas.

Missed opportunity

Although the teacher has planned a full explanation of the different grade bands, many pupils find it difficult to take in all this information without something concrete to base it on.

The tweak

This is an opportunity for you to show the class exemplar work at different levels and ask them to use the criteria to distinguish, for example, a D from a C grade piece of work. Alternatively, you could model a specific skill that determines the difference between grades.

Missed opportunity

The teacher should perhaps rethink the pairings for the peer assessment activity. If pupils are working in friendship pairs, this can affect the quality of the peer conversation. In particular, girls often seem to care more about praising the work of their friend, rather than pointing out what could be done to improve the work. In other cases, several able pairs didn't go beyond saying that they liked what their peer had done and they did not provide the pertinent feedback that the pupils need.

The tweak

As Berger discusses in *An ethic of excellence*, it is important to develop a culture where critique is not just kind, but also helpful and specific, and this takes an investment of time. You need to plan how to share and develop effective success criteria with pupils and allocate time to model what excellent peer feedback looks like, highlighting examples of effective peer-to-peer critique conversations.

In summary. . .

In a very mixed class, you will be planning for a wide spectrum of abilities. It could be quite challenging to get such a mix of pupils to interact with each other and feel confident sharing their work. This sort of environment is wholly necessary if excellent AfL practice is to take place, and the pupils need to be supported to develop knowledge of the specific success criteria and what a successful piece of work looks like. Assessment of work that features dialogue, as opposed to just written feedback, helps pupils to progress further in the long term.

Top tweaks checklist: AfL

- Provide a range of differentiated learning outcomes for pupils to choose from which are appropriate for their target grade.
- Model the difference between good and inadequate peer assessment to ensure the pupils' comments are helpful and meaningful.
- Lead the class in co-constructing the success criteria for the task, ensuring that the language is age-appropriate.
- Break up longer tasks with a peer assessment pit stop to give pupils enough time to make changes based on their peer's suggestions.
- Direct pupils to look at their criteria if they are working for extended periods of time independently to ensure they have a sense of how well they are progressing.
- Provide exemplar pieces of work for pupils to level and support them to make the correct judgement about their work.
- Provide sufficient time and resources (such as sentence stems and pupil-friendly criteria) to support pupils in developing quality peer-to-peer conversations about their work.
- Collect self-assessment information (for example using sticky notes) at the end of a lesson to help with further planning and intervention.

- A basic activity, suitable for teachers starting out with AfL, would be to give staff two variations on the same activity or lesson plan and ask them to identify why one is better than the other. Examples might include: starting the lesson by copying down the learning objective compared with giving pupils the learning objective as a series of jumbled words that they have to rearrange to make sense; or giving learning outcomes in the 'must, should, could' format compared with giving pupils three outcomes and they decide which they think is the easiest to the most challenging.

- Give participants success criteria in exam board style language for a range of subjects (not their own subject specialism) and ask them to rewrite them in pupil friendly language. They can then discuss how easy this would be for pupils to do and strategies they could use to help pupils with this.

- Give out lesson plan snippets describing activities that pupils are given relating to the learning objectives and outcomes. Participants are asked to consider how these activities could be tweaked to ensure pupils actively engage with the objectives, so that they provide opportunities to challenge all pupils or so that you can check that pupils actually understand what success against the outcomes will look like.

- SOLO taxonomy is a very useful tool to use to plan success criteria and to support a progress dialogue with pupils. A simple activity to introduce staff to this tool would be to show a real lesson example of descriptors for the four levels of the taxonomy (see online resources and appendix 1) and activities that pupils would complete according to the level they are starting at. There are books and Web-based resources available to help explain SOLO taxonomy if you would like to develop this area in more depth, for example James Atherton (learningandteaching.info, 'SOLO taxonomy.') or Pam Hook (pamhook.com, 'SOLO Taxonomy').

- It is definitely worth investing some departmental training time for building and collating a bank of exemplar work at a range of levels. The exemplars can be used in a range of ways in lessons as well as to train new staff joining the department.

- Moderator feedback and examiner's reports are often overlooked, as they tend to arrive when there are so many other priorities. The detailed breakdown of specific sections or parts of questions can be invaluable. It can be used in departments to adapt schemes of work, to create extra exemplars or other resources to support pupils or to plan lesson activities for pupils to focus on common errors or missed marks.

Assessment for Learning

- Ask your group of staff to design an enquiry question to investigate their own practice for a term or longer. Staff could observe each other in pairs or triads to focus on a very specific aspect of AfL in their classroom. Enquiry questions are most effective when they focus on a specific aspect and a specific group of pupils. Examples of enquiry questions could be: 'How can I check that my Year 9 class understand the success criteria?' or 'Which strategies are effective for ensuring my Year 11 class have sufficiently challenging learning outcomes?' The evidence to help answer their question could include evidence of coaching conversations with colleagues following lesson observations, examples of pupils' work, lesson or homework resources and feedback from interviews with pupils.

3 Questioning

(Not to be confused with asking pupils to guess the answer you already have in your head...)

Without doubt, asking the right sorts of questions is the key to helping your pupils make the most progress. Questioning is therefore a vital part of your teaching repertoire. Without interesting questions, there can be no thoughtful discussion. Without teachers modelling what excellent questioning sounds like, pupils cannot begin to question each other effectively. In the best lessons, the observer will see a range of questioning techniques being used by teachers and pupils. Although there is a place for the well-known IRF (**I**nitiation by teacher, **R**esponse by pupil, **F**eedback by teacher) technique, it should not dominate the lesson. Why? If this is the dominant technique, then the lesson cannot be pupil-centred and the teacher becomes the 'sage on the stage', demanding the answers to the questions posed. Moreover, the questions that tend to be asked with this technique are often less exploratory, meaning less thinking by the pupils takes place. The environment that we should be aiming for is the dialogic classroom, where pupils question each other at length and respond well to probing questions and the teacher plays their part in facilitating this kind of forum rather than being the sole questioner. For a more detailed discussion of dialogic teaching, read Robin Alexander's book, *Towards dialogic teaching: Rethinking classroom talk.*

In this chapter, you will see teachers using a range of questioning techniques to try and move the learning forward for their pupils. However, there will be ways in which the use of questions could be developed to improve the pupils' learning. The 'tweak' will place emphasis on getting pupils to feel confident posing their own questions and for the role of the teacher to move constantly between the master of knowledge and a learner themselves. The more questions a pupil asks, the more curious they are about the learning. An observer will want to experience an atmosphere where questions are encouraged. After all, as Albert Einstein said: 'The important thing is not to stop questioning.'

Questioning to encourage pupils to think deeply

There will be times during a lesson when you just need to check that the pupils have understood something new that you've introduced. However, there are other times when you will want to give the pupils an opportunity to explore, interpret and think insightfully about a topic. When planning a lesson, ensure sufficient thinking and/or discussion time is built in for questions that require deep thinking.

Lesson snippet 1

Lesson context: Year 10 Art and design, mixed ability class

Pupils are coming to the end of their topic and are preparing to analyse an artist's work. On the board is a selection of questions to encourage the pupils to consider the artist's work. The questions all begin with 'What' or 'How'. The pupils are asked to categorise the questions into the following areas of the analysis: form; context; content; process. Once the pupils have sorted the questions, they are then asked to rank them in the chronological order of how they would discuss them in their analysis. The teacher tells them that this series of questions will support them in structuring their paragraphs, and that if they know the answers to these questions, then they already have half of their analysis done; however, pupils will still need to evaluate if they are to get into the top band of the mark scheme. The pupils are given a few minutes to look at all of the questions they know they need to respond to in the analysis before trying to finish each paragraph by answering a 'What if?' question. Pupils can choose to work individually or in pairs to create a 'What if?' question for each of the areas of analysis. Pupils share their 'What if?' questions and the teacher selects one of them and models how they might begin responding to a question of this type.

The tweak

Make the thinking process visible by connecting lower-order questions to build up evaluative questioning.

There is no point asking pupils to think deeply unless they have already built up a bank of knowledge that they will be able to draw upon. If pupils are asked lots of 'What if?' questions too early on then their responses can be fairly lacklustre. You need knowledge to think conceptually; the more knowledge you have, the more enlightened your thinking. The lesson in the example is structured well to allow the pupils to remind themselves of what they have covered during the topic. They are consolidating their knowledge at this point; they are preparing themselves to begin to think originally. Framing a question using 'What if?' reminds the pupils that there are multiple responses and that their response to the artist's work is subjective. It is important that the teacher models this process with the pupils so they can see her thinking aloud whilst she shares the different ways she could respond to a 'What if?' question. By finishing their paragraphs with this type of evaluative questioning, the pupils have a good chance of evidencing the top band of the mark scheme.

The big idea – Questioning
Shaun Allison (classteaching.wordpress.com) 30 June 2013.

Lesson snippet 2

Lesson context: Year 7 English, low ability class

Pupils read a poem as a class. Each poem has four questions written in the margin which are based on understanding the narrative of the poem, the central character's personality and the meaning of specific words. The teacher leads a whole class discussion with the aim of ensuring that pupils are able to answer the four questions. Once the teacher is confident that pupils have understood key ideas and words in the poem, he brings out a set of envelopes labelled A B C D, each with a question inside it. The teacher makes it clear that all of the questions are exploratory and pupils must think hard before beginning to answer them. Pupils are told they must not share their question with anyone and they are given ten minutes to construct an answer. After ten minutes, pupils are paired up with another pupil who has answered a different letter. Pupils read what their peers have written. On the front of the envelope, pupils write what they think the question their peer has been answering might be. The teacher then reveals what the original questions were.

The tweak

Work backwards by guessing the question for selected answers.

Any teacher who has had experience of teaching a low ability class knows all too well that getting some pupils to think deeply can be like getting blood out of a stone! Yet ask a low ability class to copy something off the board neatly into their books and they often jump at the chance. Why? Well, there is a sense of achievement in completing a task and it is really easy. The easy route to take when teaching low ability groups is to plan lessons where the questions remain relatively easy, the pupils answer them correctly and everyone feels like progress is being made; the challenge is to take a risk and give pupils the chance to think for themselves. At first, pupils who are not used to being challenged in this way may find it difficult to engage with the demands of exploratory questioning. However, as with most things, once pupils understand that you have high expectations, they will begin to rise to the challenge if there is appropriate scaffolding. In this instance, the teacher has given his pupils a sense of security by providing questions on the poetry handout. The pressure of getting the answer to the question in the envelop wrong is decreased by the pupils being explicitly told that the questions are open-ended with no wrong answer. It is up to their peers to try and guess the correct question rather than critique their partner's answer. It is our experience that pupils in low ability classes need to feel safe before they will expose any weaknesses in themselves and begin to engage with questions that require deeper thinking. The way this task is structured supports the pupils to have a go at responding to questions that, if presented to them in a normal format, would most likely have been left unanswered.

Lesson snippet 3

Lesson context: Year 8 Religious education, mixed ability class

Pupils read a handout which describes three different perspectives on the creation of man. After reading the handout, pupils are allocated a different perspective. They are then given five minutes of thinking time on their tables to create three questions they would ask a person who held this particular belief. Once the tables have devised their three questions, they come to the board and write them out for all of the class to see. The teacher then looks through all of the questions for the three different perspectives. Pupils are asked to discuss which question for each perspective they think is the most difficult to answer. After pupils have voted, the most difficult question for each perspective is selected and pupils write individually in their books, attempting to answer the three questions.

The tweak

Get pupils to rank the level of difficulty when constructing questions.

This lesson snippet clearly demonstrates this teacher's desire for her pupils to grapple with difficult new knowledge but then apply this knowledge by thinking deeply about what they have read. It would have been easy for the teacher to provide a series of questions that increased in difficulty, but in this lesson the onus is on the pupils to consider what they need to know in order to get a better understanding of the subtleties between the oppositional perspectives. This part of the lesson is made even more challenging because the pupils have to discuss which question would be the most difficult to answer. In order for this to be a successful task, pupils will have to draw upon their new knowledge and then begin to make connections between the new knowledge to answer the most difficult questions. Finishing the task by making pupils work individually to get their answers down on paper is an opportunity for pupils to structure their thoughts in a coherent manner.

Can I be that little bit better at ... asking effective questions?
David Fawcett (reflectionsofmyteaching.blogspot.co.uk) 5 August 2014.

Thought bombing
Lisa Jane Ashes (thelearninggeek.com) 27 August 2013.

Questioning to check understanding

An excellent teacher is one that knows when their pupils understand something and are ready to move on or when they are faltering and the lesson needs to be modified. There is absolutely no point in ploughing on regardless with your planned lesson if most of the pupils have too many misconceptions about what you're teaching them. When planning, think about the points in the lesson when you will need to take a temperature check of what pupils have understood. Then consider what questions you will need to ask quickly to ascertain whether it's the right time to move on.

Lesson snippet 1

Lesson context: Year 12 Geography, mixed ability class

Pupils enter the room and look at a dot map of Brazil's population. The teacher asks pupils to use their iPads to logon to Socrative and enter his room. The teacher has preloaded a series of questions based on the dot map – there is a combination of multiple choice questions and free text responses. The teacher displays the pupils' answers on the whiteboard. There is one question that the majority of pupils have chosen the wrong answer for. He uses these wrong answers to begin a discussion on what knowledge the pupils were drawing upon to make that assumption. After the class discussion, the teacher poses a new question based on a new stimulus, using a similar format to the one the pupils answered incorrectly to check they have understood where they went wrong.

The tweak

Share pupils' misconceptions with the whole class and use as a stimulus for discussion.

Many teachers still feel uncomfortable using technology in their classrooms because of all the things that could go wrong. However, in our experience, Socrative is an easy, accessible website that can be accessed via a computer, on an iPad as an app or on a smartphone. Since it can be used across platforms, teachers are able to ask pupils to use a variety of devices to answer the preloaded questions on Socrative. The teacher in the example uses this routine at the start of each lesson in the run up to the geographical skills exam. Pupils know automatically that they will be quizzed, based on what they have learnt in the previous lesson. The ease with which the teacher is able to display the results of the pupils' answers helps to generate a useful discussion and clear up any misconceptions quickly before moving onto new material.

Lesson snippet 2

Lesson context: Year 9 Maths, middle ability class

Pupils are working on ratio and proportion; they have been working individually on a series of questions to answer. The teacher pauses and asks pupils to look at the board. On the board is a question related to ratio and proportion. Underneath the question are two different answers; only one answer is correct. Pupils are asked which answer they think is correct and why; they are given five minutes to discuss this in pairs before voting. Pupils vote and then the teacher selects two pupils who have chosen different answers to come up to the board and demonstrate how they got to their answer. As it becomes clear that one of the pupils is right and one is wrong, the teacher asks the pupil who answered correctly where they think the other pupil went wrong. All pupils in the class are then shown another problem and use mini whiteboards to display their answer.

The tweak

Allocate enough time in the lesson for pupils to assess different answers to a question.

One of the key things that excellent teachers do is to know when to stop the lesson and check that pupils have understood a new idea or concept. The key thing is to not check understanding too soon; give pupils some time to struggle before doing a whole class check. Signs to look out for are fidgeting, more than a few hands up or passivity. When you gauge the feeling in the room to be at a point where the work is bordering on too challenging, stop and bring them back together as a class. In this example, the pupils are asked which answer they think is correct. By bringing up two pupils to actively model and demonstrate how they would work out the answer, it is easy for the other pupils to see how and where you could go wrong, resulting in an incorrect answer. Whilst the two pupils are at the board, the teacher is free to scan the room and see who is still struggling; the teacher will then be able to go to help the small number of pupils when the rest of the class return to their new problem.

Better questioning: Thinking about thinking
Dan Brinton (belmontteach.wordpress.com) 23 January 2014.

Why use multiple-choice questions?
Joe Kirby (pragmaticreform.wordpress.com) 8 March 2014.

Lesson snippet 3

Lesson context: Year 11 Music, mixed ability class

Pupils have been working on their composition unit. The pupils have been exposed to a range of compositions, some more familiar than others. To check their understanding of the elements of composition, including tempo, dynamics and harmony, the teacher asks pupils to listen to a ten-minute video where a composer discusses eight elements of musical composition. The pupils have a sheet with question prompts to help them take useful notes. After the video, pupils get into groups of four to play a game of Jeopardy! The teacher gives the pupils five minutes to look over their notes and discuss in their groups anything that they are unsure of after watching the video. Once the pupils have looked over their notes and discussed information with their group, the teacher begins the game. Pupils see an answer and they have to construct the correct question. In Round 1, there is only one correct question for the displayed answer but in Round 2, there is more than one possible question the pupils could create as a match.

The tweak

Add an element of fun to answering questions by setting up a game show task.

The tasks in the example above show that you can check pupils' understanding whilst pupils are enjoying themselves by playing a game. However, the game is only a success because the pupils have taken thorough notes whilst watching the informative video. Rather than asking pupils to take notes, which is far too unstructured, question prompts is an important scaffold to ensure pupils note down the most important information. Allowing pupils time to digest their notes and speak to their peers before starting the game is another opportunity for pupils to make sense of their knowledge. There is no point checking understanding if they haven't had time to think about what they've heard. Strictly speaking, the game Jeopardy! isn't posing questions to check understanding but it is more difficult than it seems because the pupils have to think quickly against the clock to decide on the correct question. Making the decision to have multiple question options in Round 2 of the game makes it much more challenging for the pupils.

> **Do they understand this well enough to move on? Introducing hinge questions**
> Harry Fletcher-Wood (improvingteaching.co.uk) 17 August 2013.

Questioning to reflect and review progress

This is an opportunity to develop a greater sense of ownership of the learning with your pupils. The focus of this type of questioning is for pupils to consider what they know and understand at a particular point in the lesson so that they can take responsibility for their next steps. This gives a more precise picture upon which the teacher can base any necessary interventions and encourages pupils to decide whether they need more support, can continue with the task as planned or perhaps whether they need a greater level of challenge.

Lesson snippet 1

Lesson context: Year 7 Science, high ability class

Pupils have been learning about food chains and webs over a series of lessons and the teacher wants them to reflect on what they have learnt as well as consider what they still need to spend time on to secure the new knowledge. Each pupil is given a blank copy of a questioning grid: prompts down the side begin with What? Why? Where? When? Who? and How? Across the top of the grid are the words: Is? Did? Will? Could? Might? and Should? Pupils are given 15 minutes to complete the 36 boxes with questions using the horizontal and vertical prompts. During this time, the teacher is scanning the room and intervening where appropriate if a pupil's questioning could be improved. Once the grids are completed, pupils are given 20 minutes to answer as many of their questions as possible. They are asked to circle questions that they do not feel completely confident answering. The teacher can use the circled questions to help her planning of the revision lesson before the test.

The tweak

Use a questioning scaffold such as John Sayers' questioning grid.

This is an excellent task for pupils in a higher ability class who can work independently for an extended period. Pupils develop their own questioning and can easily review their progress by how well they answer the questions. The pupils lead this task, which allows the teacher to support those who need extra input and perhaps are struggling to formulate questions that require more higher-order thinking. Furthermore, asking the pupils to circle the questions that they do not feel confident they would be able to answer fully in the upcoming test is a great way for the teacher to modify her planning to ensure her pupils are best prepared for the test. If there is a pattern in the type of questions pupils are circling, then the teacher can plan a lesson based upon these questions; if only a few pupils seem to have difficulty in a particular area, then they can be given extra resources or directed to a website to aid them with their revision.

Lesson snippet 2

Lesson context: Year 10 Sociology, mixed ability class

Pupils are halfway through their crime and deviance topic. As soon as they enter the room, a statement is displayed on the board. Pupils are given a Bloom's taxonomy pyramid with question stems. The teacher asks pupils to consider what questions they would have to ask in order to conclude an essay on the statement on the board. Pupils are put into mixed ability groups of six, with each pupil responsible for coming up with two questions for their level of the pyramid. Once pupils have decided on their questions, they then share them with their group and decide on the order they would bring these questions into their essay. Each group then writes out the order of the questions they would respond to in their essay on a piece of A3 paper and sticks it up around the room for other groups to see. The teacher then asks the pupils to go around the gallery and think which essay has got the best questions in it, which should lead to a well-argued essay. After looking at all groups' questions, the teacher then reveals the questions she would want to tackle if she were to write an essay in response to this question.

The tweak

Construct an extended piece of writing by using a series of linked questions.

This method of planning a piece of extended writing is an effective method for the teacher to try and see into the pupils' brains and get a sense of not only what information they have remembered but also what they deem as relevant. Asking pupils to plan an extended essay can fill some with dread at such a daunting task, but breaking it down into a series of questions to consider makes the task seem much more manageable. Giving the pupils an opportunity for them to see if their questions are similar or different to their peers is a helpful way for pupils to monitor their own progress. Following this up with the teacher revealing which questions she believes to be most pertinent is another opportunity for the pupils to judge how much they know about crime and deviance. If the pupils' questions are too basic or missing a particular aspect of the topic, then the teacher knows they are not ready to tackle the exam essay question and will need further teaching.

Questioning – Top ten strategies
Alex Quigley (huntingenglish.com) 10 November 2012.

Lesson snippet 3

Lesson context: Year 11 German, mixed ability class

The teacher wants the pupils to review their progress in the topic 'My holidays', which they will have to write about for their assessment. The teacher asks pupils to complete a KWL (What do I know? What do I want to know? What have I learnt?) grid at different points in the lesson. The pupils begin by completing the first column: 'What do I know?' Pupils are able to use any resources they have available which they think will help them. Pupils then get into pairs, then fours, to compare existing knowledge. Next, pupils are asked to complete the middle column: 'What do I want to know?' Pupils are asked to also write this information on a sticky note and stick it on a display board. To help pupils, the teacher displays on the board detailed and specific requirements for an A* assessment. At this point, the teacher looks at all of the sticky notes and then splits the room into three workshop areas with different tasks and resources based on what the pupils said they wanted to know. At the end of the lesson, the pupils will have to complete the final column 'What have I learnt?' after they have spent time in their workshop area.

The tweak

Pupils choose their own tasks based on their prior knowledge and what they want to learn during the lesson.

Reviewing progress by asking the pupils the KWL questions is an easy way to respond to the needs of pupils and differentiate your lesson accordingly. The first column helps the teacher to identify the strengths of the teaching sequence based on the pupils' acquisition of new knowledge. The second column should not be a total surprise for the teacher as it should be based on the criteria for the assessment. Excellent teachers already have a sense of where in the teaching sequence pupils have struggled to understand and apply something new. The second column allows the teacher to respond to the weaknesses of different pupils by setting up the resourced workshop areas. The third column, which is completed at the end of the lesson, is a good way for pupils to judge what skills and knowledge they have acquired as they work towards their assessment.

The problem with progress part 3: Designing lessons for learning
David Didau (learningspy.co.uk) 16 February 2013.

Kate Butrie's show call & the 'Invisible hand'
A Guest Post by Joaquin Hernandez. Doug Lemov (teachlikeachampion.com) 31 January 2014.

Peer-to-peer questioning

Often teachers can forget how difficult it is for young people to have the confidence and know-how to speak at length. We assume that because pupils enjoy talking to their friends, they will automatically use these skills in the formal setting of a classroom. The loudest of pupils can clam up when asked to get into a structured discussion with their peers – particularly, if they are sat next to pupils who are not in their friendship circle. To overcome these barriers, it is vital that we explicitly teach pupils how to ask and respond to thoughtful questions in order to enhance their knowledge and understanding.

Lesson snippet 1

Lesson context: Year 12 Media arts, mixed ability class

Pupils are learning about the changing nature of the video game industry. Pupils have been asked to come up with a hypothesis about what the industry will look like in 15 years. Pupils are given 20 minutes to construct a presentation where they put forward their hypothesis based on case studies and other research. After each presentation, an audience member asks questions based on Socratic questioning. Questions that the pupil is asked to consider are: Why have you come to this conclusion? Is this always the case? Is there any other information you have not used that might develop your argument? What might be an alternative way of looking at this? How might X affect Y? Why do you think my line of questioning is important for your argument? After each exchange, the teacher gives the speaker feedback on the quality of their argument and how they responded to Socratic questioning.

The tweak

Use Socratic questioning to develop pupils' ability to challenge their peers' thinking.

Socratic questioning is a very structured way of probing pupils' thinking. It should be modelled by the teacher first so pupils have a good example in their head. This type of questioning is quite lengthy and needs enough time allocated for it to be anything but superficial, so it works best with a smaller class or as a starter or plenary between two pupils who hold opposing views. At each stage, the pupil presenting has to think carefully about how to respond. The pupil will be challenged and errors in their thinking may be exposed. This is not only to be expected but also encouraged because the point of Socratic questioning is not to win the argument but to be sure you have considered all angles in order to have a concrete argument. This type of questioning aims to be dispassionate, concentrating on the information provided – some pupils might find this structured questioning difficult to keep to without going off on a tangent or becoming too emotional!

Lesson snippet 2

Lesson context: Year 10 Business studies, mixed ability class

The teacher has chosen to use Philosophy for Children as a way for pupils to consider the ethical issues surrounding large chains changing the face of a high street that used to have many small businesses. The teacher begins by sharing the stimulus: a clip from BBC News about the declining state of the high street which includes interviews with a small business owner who cannot afford the rent for his shop, and a director of a large retail business that is planning to open later in the year. After the pupils have watched the stimulus, they sit in a circle and write an exploratory question that they would like to discuss on a Post-it note and put it into a box passed around the class. The teacher reads out all of the questions, the pupils vote for their preferred choice and then begin their discussion of: 'Is it acceptable for retail chains to outnumber small businesses if there are empty shops on the high street?' There is a small soft ball that pupils must have in their possession if they are to contribute to the discussion. The teacher appoints a pupil to chair the discussion who begins by inviting a member of the class to share their views. When the pupil has finished, they then bounce the ball to another pupil to develop the argument. Once all members of the class have contributed to the discussion, the teacher then asks each pupil to vote 'yes' or 'no' based on the chosen question at the start of the session.

The tweak

Use Philosophy for Children as a structured way to teach pupils how to discuss and debate.

Philosophy for Children is a discussion technique that can be used successfully across the curriculum. All you need to set it up are engaging stimuli, laminated question stem cards to prompt pupils who may find it difficult to share their opinions and an appointed chairperson. Explain that it is a democratic space and all opinions and ideas are welcomed. It encourages pupils to create interesting, exploratory questions as well as gain confidence in responding to their peers' ideas. It is important that the teacher is not the chairperson because then pupils look to the teacher for the 'correct' answer. Philosophy for Children is something that works best when it is well planned; just because pupils might talk to each other in the playground doesn't mean they can magically talk at length in the more formal setting of a classroom. Laminating and providing the pupils with the question stem cards means there is no reason why someone should opt out of the discussion if they can't think of a question to ask someone in the circle. To become familiar with how to interact in the circle, pupils will need several attempts at practising: posing a question; waiting an appropriate time before expecting responses; selecting a pupil to begin the discussion then drawing in others who could contribute further.

Lesson snippet 3

Lesson context: Year 7 Design and technology, mixed ability class
Pupils are at the initial design stage of their graphics project where the outcome is to make a wrapper for a new food product. Pupils have carried out some research into the market and have created their first design. They are now ready to get some feedback from their peers about their initial design. Pupils are put into groups of three, with each pupil taking on the role of a young child, a supermarket owner or a parent. Pupils are given five minutes to write down the two questions they will ask the designer about their food wrapper. When the pupils have their questions, the designer is asked four questions in total. The designer responds to them in their role, taking into account who they are and their responses to the initial design. Once each designer has interacted with two of their peers, they then write up feedback they have received and possible changes they may need to make to their design.

The tweak

Use role play to develop pupils' confidence when giving feedback on their peers' work.

This is a twist on the usual WWW/EBI models of peer feedback. The teacher has decided to give the pupils a role whilst giving feedback because several pupils in this Year 7 class lack confidence in their work and may react negatively if they feel their work is being criticised. Distancing the person from the feedback by turning it into role play can be an effective strategy to support pupils in accepting feedback from their peers. In addition, there is a tendency amongst younger pupils to repeat the same feedback that has already been said. In this case, the pupils have to think about the design from a certain perspective and so the questions they will ask the designer will most likely be different, leading to richer feedback. It is important that the teacher has built in time for pupils to consider what questions would be most appropriate for them to ask based on the role they have been given; otherwise, some pupils may have drawn a blank and been unable to participate.

5 techniques for questioning in your classroom
Mark Anderson (ictevangelist.com) 15 December 2013.

Pose, pause, pounce, bounce!
Ross Morrison McGill (teachertoolkit.me) 4 January 2013.

Questioning
John Sayers (sayersjohn.blogspot.co.uk) 6 January 2013.

Annotated Design and technology lesson plan

START HERE

Where does this lesson fit into the topic?

Design, build and evaluate a wooden box:
7 of 10

What is the key learning question?

Which techniques are most effective to make my box?

Where are students in the independent cycle?

Explaining
Modelling
(Scaffolding)
Practising

Differentiated outcomes

1. Construct a box & explain techniques used
2. Construct a well-joined box & evaluate techniques used
3. Add a precise finish & explain how to produce different effects

The hook

Identify the tool (warm)/
explain it's function (hot)

Warm task(s)

- Practical tasks with teacher support
- Reflection task to identify next steps & techniques needed to achieve them
- Homework: to research uses of your type of box

Hot task(s)

- Practical independently
- Reflection task to identify next steps & techniques needed to achieve them
- Homework: to think of a new use for your type of box

Scorching task(s)

- Practical task with technician
- Reflection task to identify next steps & techniques needed to achieve them

Pupils are provided with instructions that are clear and pupil-friendly so that they can work independently.

Extended practical projects can be excuses for pupils to waste time. Planning time for target setting keeps pupils on track and helps the teacher to monitor progress each lesson.

Monitoring progress points

1. Hook: Pupil B marks A, T marks B
2. T questions lower ability pupils
3. T reads peer checklists once completed
4. T reads reflections as pupils pack away

Groupings

Individual
- Reflection task

Pair
- Hook task
- Peer assessment

Group
- Ability groups of 4 for practical work

The teacher uses the more able pupils (B) to mark their partner's work (A), freeing up the teacher to mark the more challenging task.

Ensure your questions are stretching pupils by asking more difficult follow-up questions when a correct answer is given. This could be as simple as 'why do you think that?'

Questions have yes/no or single word answers, so the feedback is easy to understand and act upon.

Key words

Corner halving joint
Butt joint
Comb joint
Coping saw
Tenon saw
Chisel

Questions to develop thinking

What skills do you have that you're not using?
Stop and look at your work: Is this in your design?

The teacher uses a 'coaching style' strategy to empower pupils to solve problems themselves rather than relying on the teacher for the answer.

The takeaway

As pupils pack away: 'Which technique is most important in producing a professional finish?'

Questioning provision in Design and technology lesson plan

- The lesson begins with a differentiated hook activity, which matches the different needs of the pupils. Less able pupils are asked to identify the tools whilst more able pupils are expected to identify their purpose.

- The teacher uses the knowledge of the more able pupils to mark the work of the less able, which frees up his time to check the understanding of the more able pupils.

- For the practical task, there is a set of clear and pupil-friendly instructions. The instructions include a series of 'quick check' questions, so that pupils can solve their own problems and check they have completed all that is necessary before moving on.

- The teacher will work mostly with the weaker pupils. He uses a coaching style of questioning to try to encourage them to become more independent and build confidence to solve their own problems.

- The reflection task, a peer assessment activity to identify the next steps, is well structured with short answer, easy to interpret questions for pupils to ask each other.

Missed opportunities and tweaks

Missed opportunity

The teacher has decided to spend all of his time with a small group of pupils. Although there is some brief monitoring of the activity, the teacher only engages fully with these few pupils. It's a catch-22 situation – the pupils work well by themselves, so why disrupt them? But if they just work quietly by themselves, how can the teacher be sure that they are really stretching themselves to the best of their ability?

The tweak

When your pupils have an extended period of time on a task, do you need to stay with those same pupils for the whole time? Perhaps after a pit stop (such as the peer assessment activity in this example), if you are confident that these pupils are making good progress, you could plan to engage with a greater range of pupils, using different levels of question to make them think more critically about what they are doing.

Missed opportunity

The main opportunity the pupils have to question each other and get into a good quality conversation in this plan is during the halfway pit stop. All pupils, regardless of their starting point, use the same series of questions that are on the board to anchor the conversation. All of the questions fall into the lower level of Bloom's taxonomy, asking pupils to identify and describe what they are doing. There are no questions that offer the pupils any chance to analyse, synthesise or evaluate. This peer assessment is planned to be in mixed ability pairings, which would make it more difficult to use more challenging questions because one of the pupils in the pair is at a much lower level than the other.

The tweak

Often, peer assessment activities work better if the pairs are of similar ability; that way, your pupils can have conversations that are pitched to their level. The questions could get progressively more challenging, which would make pupils more engaged during the peer assessment activity. You could encourage the most able pupils to generate their own questions, giving them a greater level of independence during the conversation.

Missed opportunity

The most exploratory, thought-provoking question is planned to be asked with only a couple of minutes to go. The highest level outcome of the lesson is about considering the effects of different techniques. The question is well pitched for this learning outcome. There are several pupils who should be aiming at this outcome but this is the only question that they will be asked (as part of a whole class discussion) to get them thinking deeply. There is no chance to interact with the teacher, who could ask probing questions, because he is working with the weaker pupils. In addition, the highest ability pupils don't have a chance to speak to each other because the peer assessment activity is done in mixed ability pairings.

The tweak

Plan more time for higher-level, exploratory questions. A better time to introduce that question is at the start of an extended task (such as the practical activity in this example). You could pose the question and tell pupils to be prepared to discuss this at a later point. This gives pupils more time to consider what their response will be and allow a greater proportion of pupils to access higher-level thinking. Even if they do not answer, they will be able to hear the responses of others and this might set off an idea of their own.

In summary...

It's a hard balance to achieve between pupils working quietly and pupils having time to talk to each other. You need to think really carefully about the range of pupils in your class when allocating enough time for appropriately challenging questions that are stimulating to pupils. It is also important to develop dialogue between pupils so that they have opportunities to discuss questions with peers of a similar ability. To increase the level of questioning, you need to plan to develop peer-to-peer questions, providing examples and question stems to support pupils as required. This is discussed further in the lesson snippets section 'Peer-to-peer questioning' (page 53).

Annotated English lesson plan

Teacher	Date and period	Subject	Class and ability range	Boy:girl ratio
Miss Starr	3/12/P4	English	Top band	14:18

Student context:	EAL	SEN	G&T
	1	2 MLD, 1 SpLD (dyslexia), 1 SLCN	0

Learning objective
To understand how Duffy presents the character of Medusa through the language she uses.

Differentiated learning outcomes
1. Explore the meaning of the character through exploring the effect of different language choices.
2. Analyse key words or phrases in the poem and the effect they have on the reader.
3. Offer an interpretation of the language used by the poet to present her character in the poem.

Resources needed
PowerPoint, key words from poem for the starter, writing scaffolds for the main activity, sticky notes.

Lesson content	Planned opportunities to check prior knowledge and further pupil progress

> This strategy ensures every pupil makes a contribution to the group task.

Starter activity
Each pupil in a group is given a statement about the poem, Medusa. Then pupils share ideas with other pupils in their group to see if their ideas are similar or different. Introduce the character of Medusa.

Teacher listens to spokespeople give feedback to gauge initial understanding of the poem.

> The use of a key question is more thought-provoking for pupils of this ability than a learning objective. Pupils are required to formulate a response to this key question.

New learning activities
Teacher introduces the key question that pupils need to respond to in the lesson: How do you think the poet wants us to respond to Medusa? Pupils decide what learning outcome they need to aim for based on their target grade.

Teacher will guide pupils in selecting the appropriate learning outcome based on their prior attainment.

Teacher reads out the poem twice using different tones. In groups, pupils discuss how their understanding of the character changed with the second reading. Teacher asks pupils to select words/phrases that they felt were read aloud differently and for what effect.

Teacher listens to the responses from the class and asks questions to probe thinking and generate a deeper understanding.

Each group is given three questions to explore:
1) Do you think Medusa is a victim or an aggressor?
2) What do you think is the most important word/phrase in the poem?
3) What point about literature might the writer be making by writing her version of the well known narrative, Medusa?

> These three questions are exploratory and provocative, so will work well for Socratic discussion.

> Pupils are actively involved in selecting their own outcome which encourages them to think more carefully about what they wish to achieve.

Lesson Planning Tweaks for Teachers

60

Lesson content			Planned opportunities to check prior knowledge and further pupil progress	
Pupils begin their whole class Socratic discussion. One pupil is asked to chair and lead the discussion and another is asked to take notes during the discussion for final reflection. ←				
Teacher returns to the key question and asks pupils to write a paragraph in response.			Teacher collects in written work in the pupils' books.	
Teacher sets homework tasks.				
Reflection activities Pit stop 1 after starter: Teacher selects spokespeople to give feedback on initial ideas.				
Pit stop 2 after Socratic discussion: The pupil taking notes gives their feedback to the class, drawing on the main ideas and conclusions of the discussion.				

Differentiation strategies used in the lesson	Through task	Through questioning all stages	Through groupings	Through teacher and other adults' support
S – Starter NL – New learning activity R – Reflection activity T – throughout.	S – Differentiated statements for pupils.	NL – Higher-order Socratic questions used by the class during whole class Socratic discussion.	S – Ability groups NL – Pupil who has SLCN takes on role as the note-taker to try and help them participate in the discussion. Most able pupil takes on role as the chair/lead.	Teacher is targeting SEN pupils during the final writing task, particularly the pupil with dyslexia who has the most difficulty with writing.

Literacy/numeracy links
Specific focus on language techniques in the poem.
Key words for poetry displayed on the Key Word Poster in the room.
Tracing patterns in rhyme and rhythm when reading the poem aloud.

Homework task
Choice of three tasks: collage; topic sentences; annotating poem and comparing to another Duffy poem. ←

Questioning provision in English lesson plan

- The introduction of a key question is more thought-provoking for a class of this ability than a learning objective. It forces pupils to formulate a response rather than just meeting an objective.

- Using a spokesperson to get feedback from each group allows pupils of all abilities to hear the thoughts of others.

- The pupils are given time to prepare for whole class discussion, which should lead to better quality discussion. The three questions that they need to prepare for are exploratory, provocative questions that will work well for a Socratic discussion.

- The use of Socratic discussion encourages the pupils to lead their own learning and take responsibility for developing their own ideas to a deeper level.

- The written paragraph answer to the key learning question will help the teacher monitor the progress the pupils are making as individuals, as well as using their contributions to the whole class discussion.

Missed opportunity

During the whole class discussion, the final question is unlikely to be discussed as the teacher will be short of time. This final question is the most interesting in some ways, because it sets the learning in a wider context. Many interesting ideas won't have the opportunity to be developed because of a lack of time. The main activity needs to be changed because there is no way that all pupils will be able to get involved in the discussion in the space of 23 minutes. Either you get 30 pupils responding in a basic and limited way or you get some pupils stealing the limelight and talking at length.

The tweak

For a group this size, you will need to plan this as a two-period lesson. Alternatively, you could reduce the number of questions to be discussed to two and have half the group participating in the discussion for the first question with the remaining pupils observing the learning, then swap over for the second question.

Missed opportunity

A large-scale discussion is a very difficult lesson to plan effectively. It is difficult to manage as the behaviour of a small number of pupils can mean the whole class discussion isn't completed properly.

The tweak

In the future, these whole class discussions would benefit from a set of rules to help pupils to behave in a way that makes for a stimulating discussion. You should develop these rules with your pupils and then display them somewhere highly visible so that they can be referred to during the discussion, if necessary. If a pupil refuses to adhere to these rules, ask them to leave the group and observe.

Missed opportunity

The written work of the pupils will not be a true indicator of the progress pupils had made against the learning objective because an inadequate amount of time is planned to complete the written activity.

The tweak

If you have a lesson where the majority of the work is presented by the pupils verbally, with careful planning this may be sufficient to monitor each pupil's progress. If so, the writing can be moved to a homework activity, giving extra time to the discussion to allow more pupils to participate. Those that reach the end of the lesson and have not participated should be identified (sensitively) and asked to offer their ideas in a small group, which you monitor, during the time when the others receive the feedback from the note-taker.

In summary...

This lesson plan is very pupil-centred; it requires the pupils to engage, respond to others, develop deep learning and learn from others. This example is an ambitious lesson plan that gives pupils responsibility for the direction of the lesson, making the learning very challenging. Don't underestimate the importance of pupil talk and its role in helping pupils to make excellent progress. A lesson of this nature needs to be planned so that there are not too many activities and questions, so that the questions cover a range of levels of difficulty and so that there are regular time checks to keep pupils on track. The more difficult the question, the more time the pupils will want to explore all the different responses to it, so consider this in your planning.

Top tweaks checklist: questioning

- Use the full range of Bloom's questions to make a range of pupils think more critically about what they are doing during a task.

- Select pairings based on similar ability if the task requires extended dialogue to ensure conversations are pitched at a suitable level.

- Ensure there is adequate time built in during a lesson for pupils to engage with the more interesting, exploratory questions.

- Pose the higher-order thinking questions, at some points, to the whole class so that less able pupils can hear some of the responses of other pupils, even if they do not have their own response.

- Extend the wait time to ensure more pupils respond to questions and that their responses are confident and impressive.

- Provide question stems or a suggested list of questions on the board in different categories of difficulty – for example, warm, hot or scorching – for pupils to choose from and ask during their discussions.

- Consider how long it takes to listen to contributions from all pupils during a whole class discussion; you may want to spread a lesson content based heavily on discussion over two periods, or have half the class observe the discussion of the other half before swapping over roles.

- Carve out clear rules for whole class discussion, which are visible at all times, to remind pupils what is expected of them – particularly if you are taking the role of another listener, rather than teacher.

Learning leader: questioning

- Before a training session on questioning, ask your staff to bring a lesson plan and register for a class they will be teaching in the following week. During the session, ask participants to think about the questions they usually ask in lessons and set them the task of planning levelled questions to target specific pupils in the class.

- Set staff a classroom-based task. Either ask them to video themselves teaching or to take their mobile device to their lesson and leave the voice recorder on during the lesson. Following the lesson, the teacher then listens to the questions they asked during the lesson. If this is set up without the teacher knowing the focus, they will get a more realistic picture of the questions they usually ask in a lesson. The follow-up would be for the teacher to carefully plan their questions for a lesson, as well as the particular pupils (or level of pupil) they will ask each question to. Ideally, this lesson (or part of a lesson) would then be observed by a colleague or filmed so that the responses of pupils to these questions can be reviewed.

- In a training session or departmental development time, construct a bank of question stems to give to pupils. These may be, for example, to start pupils off on a discussion, to help them to constructively challenge one another or to probe each other's thinking during a verbal planning session. These can then be used as a starting point in lessons to improve questioning between pupils.

- Hinge questions are so useful to identify misconceptions and check understanding rather than just recall. They are difficult to write but just one hinge question can make a lesson much more effective, because hinge questions are designed to check exactly what pupils understand (and specific misconceptions they may have) to help the teacher decide where the lesson needs to go next. These are well explained by Harry Fletcher-Wood (see blog link on page 49). One way these could be developed is using department development time. Staff choose a key concept in their subject that pupils struggle with and work backwards by considering what the possible misconceptions could be and using those to write multiple choice answers to a question. Once this tricky task has been achieved, staff consider the tasks pupils would need to do if they selected each of the four available answers. For example, if a pupil answers A, they have the correct answer so they can progress on to task 1; if a pupil gives B as an answer, they probably have a certain misconception and need to complete task 2, and so on.

- Suggested staff enquiry questions for questioning could include: How can I improve the quality of questions that pupils in my class ask each other? or Which questioning techniques encourage my pupils to give more detailed answers?

4 Stretch and challenge

(Not just giving the clever ones more exercises to get on with to keep them quiet...)

In the past, lesson plans often included the 'All, Most, Some' approach whereby a teacher would plan low-level tasks that every pupil in the class would be expected to complete, some slightly more challenging tasks for the majority to complete and tasks that would only be completed by the most able. This could mean the brighter pupils, who are capable of completing all three levels, might feel hard done by ('Why should I do more just because I'm clever?') or simply lack the motivation to do any more than what is expected of 'all' learners. It also meant that pupils tended to see themselves as falling within a particular band in the class and got used to aiming to just complete the lowest level tasks each lesson.

Thankfully, this practice is now seen as rather outdated, particularly when you read the Ofsted framework and its insistence that all pupils are given the opportunity to make better than expected progress. Therefore, rather than specifying that the most able learners are sufficiently challenged, teachers are planning to ensure that tasks are sufficiently challenging for *all* learners regardless of their learning needs. This, in effect means that 'stretch and challenge' now encompasses differentiation as well as meeting the needs of all pupils whether they are gifted and talented, have special educational needs or have English as an additional language.

In the classroom, this means that lessons are planned to ensure that all learners have opportunities to be stretched and challenged and that the teacher intervenes within lessons to ensure this is happening. Teachers will continue to provide support for specific groups of pupils, however they may make this support available in different ways, for example by giving pupils a choice of which resources they decide to use and when they need them.

Teachers may need to adjust their responses to struggling pupils to allow them to experience what Robert Bjork refers to as 'desirable difficulties' (Bjork, 2013); that is, a level of challenge in an activity that supports learning. He states that: 'the conditions of learning need to induce encoding and retrieval processes that are substantial and varied, and incorporating desirable difficulties helps to induce those processes.' (Bjork, 2013). This can be a difficult shift for a teacher to make, so it is important to equip our pupils with strategies to deal with getting stuck and frustrated, particularly those pupils who are not used to failing. Bjork also highlights the importance of remembering that we need to take care not to produce difficulties that are undesirable: 'a given learner is not equipped to overcome a difficulty that would otherwise be desirable, it becomes an undesirable difficulty.' (Bjork, 2013)

As Tom Sherrington (@headguruteacher) writes, we need to develop 'a belief that thinking and struggling are prerequisites for learning and that there is nothing to fear.'

Grouping strategies

One of the perennial dilemmas for all teachers is where best to sit pupils. Should they sit in rows or groups? If they sit in groups, how many on a table? Should they sit in mixed ability groups or with pupils of similar ability? How best can the teacher move around and support pupils who need more help? These are the questions that buzz around a teacher's head when making their seating plan and thinking about the best way to structure activities. There is no hard and fast rule about the best way to group your pupils, but flexibility is key; just because you made a seating plan in September, doesn't mean it has to stay that way in every lesson for the whole year. Mix it up when necessary.

Lesson snippet 1

Lesson context: Year 12 Psychology, mixed ability class

Pupils are to spend the lesson reading case studies in preparation for their 'Core studies' exam. Pupils are split into groups of three and each group is given a different case study. The teacher assigns a role to each pupil: summariser; critic; case studies linker. Each group has a blank table with three columns ready to be filled in once they have read the case study: the first pupil summarises key findings under 'Summary'; the second pupil highlights weaknesses in the investigation under 'Weaknesses'; the third pupil makes connections to other case studies under 'Links to other cases'. Once the tables are complete, the teacher takes pictures of them on his iPad and shares them with the pupils via Google Drive.

The tweak

Create a sense of collective responsibility by assigning different roles to pupils.

When deciding on appropriate groupings, ask yourself what is the point of having pupils work with each other. There is a difference between sitting in groups and working in groups.

In this example, each pupil has a clear role so they know why they are working together. The teacher has realised that pupils are struggling to read and absorb all the case studies they need to learn for their exam so has decided that they will need to support each other and has tweaked his seating plans accordingly. Pupils know that they are working in these groups for the next four weeks; the onus is on each pupil to contribute to ensure that the notes are of a high enough quality for revision. Although the pupils are working in groups, they are really working as a whole class because they need to know all the case studies.

Make sure that your pupils know what their role is and why it is so important that they contribute to a task.

Lesson snippet 2

Lesson context: Year 11 Media arts, mixed ability class

Pupils enter the room. Next to the interactive whiteboard there is a large A3 plan showing two seating plans: one seating plan is based on mixed ability groupings, which are the 'home' tables; the other is based on similar ability groupings, which are 'away' tables. The teacher has labelled the 'home' and 'away' seating plans as MTV tables and YouTube tables. A task is displayed on the board: 'A group discussion of: why do we need censorship for music videos that feature sexually explicit content?' Underneath the task, the phrase 'MTV tables' is written. Pupils go to their 'home tables' and begin their discussion, with the teacher gaining feedback from a spokesperson from each group. After the discussion, the next task is displayed on the board: 'Write a persuasive letter to the British Board of Film Classification arguing either for or against a change in the rules for broadcasting music videos.' Underneath the task, the phrase, 'YouTube tables' is written. Pupils change into their new 'away table' groups and begin planning and drafting their responses.

The tweak

Use 'home and away' tables to give pupils the opportunity to work with pupils of similar and different abilities.

Many teachers start the year with good intentions about using seating plans more effectively. We try out a couple of different seating plans, find one that we are comfortable with and keep it for the rest of the year. Unfortunately, this approach means there are many missed opportunities to use groupings effectively to promote challenge in the classroom. One reason seating plans often stay the same is because moving tables around takes so much time. However, this approach requires no movement of tables; what it does require is very careful planning and clear communication of seating to the pupils.

In this example, the teacher changes his seating plan at the end of each topic, with each topic lasting approximately every half term. The table names are linked to the topic the pupils are studying – in this case MTV and YouTube. The MTV tables represent mixed ability groups and the YouTube tables represent ability groups. The teacher has thought carefully about the types of tasks his pupils will do and has made the decision for discussion activities to take place in mixed-ability groups but writing or producing tasks in ability groups. Having two different seating plans means your pupils can be challenged in different ways.

We think it is a good idea to review your seating plans after each major assessment so that pupils are used to working with different pupils and are exposed to new ideas and perspectives. Although on paper pupils may be considered a similar ability, their level or exam target grade does not reveal the areas they need to improve. Two pupils might be working at a B grade, but their competency against the different skill descriptors or exam assessment objectives will likely be different.

Stretch and challenge

Lesson snippet 3

Lesson context: Year 9 English, middle ability class

In this class, the pupils are competing in a league. There are 14 teams in the league (28 pupils in the class). The pupils are studying *Much ado about nothing*. The teams get points for the quality of their learning in the hooks, plenaries and homeworks. This includes the following tasks: translating Shakespearean language into modern day English; role play; analysis writing; creative writing; vocabulary and punctuation worksheets; asking good questions. Two routines happen in this class; first, at the end of the week, pupils are given their match report to complete, where they evidence where they think they have accrued points for their team based on the hooks, plenaries and homeworks; secondly, at the start of each week, the teacher displays the league table to show the positions of the different teams.

The tweak

Create a class league table to identify and celebrate excellent learning.

Setting up a league table will only work if the teacher is committed to monitoring the pupils' efforts and awarding the points regularly. The pupils need to take it seriously and buy into it if there is to be any increase in their appetite to be challenged.

It is unrealistic to think that this will work with every class but in this example the teacher has chosen to do this with her Year 9 class who have become a bit uninterested with many of them only doing the bare minimum required – they are coasting. The teacher has made a number of decisions to make the league table work as a useful addition to her normal lesson planning. First, she has decided to have mixed ability pairs in each team because a number of skills are being assessed so working in ability pairs is not necessary. Secondly, the teams can only get points for the hooks, plenaries and homeworks – the main part of the lesson is still focused on pupils working individually to develop their learning. This is important because in the teacher's routine there is always a part of the lesson for some quiet, individual writing or reading which she assesses to judge whether they are making good learning gains. The league table does not interfere with her routine. Thirdly, introducing homeworks as a way of picking up points has led to an increase in quality because the pupils do not want to let their team members down. Finally, asking the pupils to reflect on their weekly contributions before she allocates points means the pupils have time to think about whether they really are putting in enough effort and responding well to being challenged.

If you find yourself with one of those classes who don't seemed to have gelled as a class or there is a general level of apathy towards learning, this element of competition could do wonders to transform the classroom environment into one where challenge is expected and embraced.

Digital debates – Classroom seating – Issue 9
Sarah Findlater (msfindlater.blogspot.co.uk) 1 February 2014.

Differentiation: Making possible the impossible
Andy Tharby (reflectingenglish.wordpress.com) 15 May 2014.

Competition vs. cooperation in the classroom
David Weller (barefooteflteacher.com)

Provision of choices

Giving pupils choices in what and how they learn is a complicated business: on paper, it seems like a good idea to give pupils ownership but the reality can be that pupils don't always make the right choices! As teachers, we should be looking for ways to support pupils in making informed choices that will help them develop their knowledge, skills and understanding. It is important to ensure that the teacher explains clearly the rationale for any choices that are available and that the teacher keeps track of the choices pupils are making in lessons.

There will always be the keen-to-please pupil who attempts a task that is much too challenging or the more able pupil who takes the easy option. This may mean that initially you need to intervene by asking a particular pupil to 'Try the first level task for today' or 'Give the scorching task a go, you need more of a challenge' until your pupils get better at making appropriate selections for themselves.

Great lessons 3: Challenge
Tom Sherrington (headguruteacher.com) 31 January 2013.

Great lessons 4: Differentiation
Tom Sherrington (headguruteacher.com) 3 February 2013.

Differentiation Part 2: What it probably is
Rachael Stevens (edulike.blogspot.co.uk) 22 October 2013.

Lesson snippet 1

Lesson context: Year 7 Art and design, mixed ability class

Pupils are working on portraits. The task is for pupils to draw their own portrait, taking inspiration from one of the artists they have been studying during the topic. On the board there is a three-column table labelled 'warm', 'hot' and 'scorching'. The warm task is for pupils to draw a face including four different features, taking inspiration from van Gogh. The hot task is to create a mixed media portrait using paint and one other medium. The scorching task is to take a portrait drawn by a pre-20th century artist and reimagine it, taking inspiration from a list of 20th century portrait artists. Pupils have five minutes to decide which task they will choose based on the feedback they have received so far during the topic and their personal preference. Each pupil writes on their mini whiteboard which task they have chosen. If the teacher is unsure about some pupils' choices then they are required to consult further with the teacher. The other pupils then regroup so that each workstation in the art studio becomes a table for the warm, hot and scorching tasks.

The tweak

Encourage pupils to aim for a high level of challenge by naming and visibly showing them the different levels of challenge.

The 'warm, hot, scorching' model allows teachers and pupils to keep a record of how much challenge a pupil is experiencing in relation to their starting point. Pupils want to try for the scorching task but they need to prove that they can successfully tackle warm and hot tasks first.

In this case, once the pupils have chosen their task, the teacher gets them to sit in a group with other pupils completing the same task. This makes it easier for them to support each other, and it also means the teacher can easily intervene and engage in dialogue with the whole group at once – they can give the same advice to a group of pupils rather than repeating themselves.

Warm, hot, scorching can also be used when everyone is working on the same task but there are different resources or levels of scaffold available.

Lesson snippet 2

Lesson context: Year 10 BTEC Health and social care, mixed ability class

Pupils begin the lesson by receiving feedback on an essay they have written on health and well-being. Attached to their essay is a copy of the marking criteria, and the teacher has highlighted where there is limited evidence that they have covered a particular criterion. The teacher explains to the pupils that none of them would have gained a distinction for their work at this point so they need to develop their essays further. To help them do this, the teacher has set up workstations around the room which focus on different aspects of the criteria. At each workstation there are several tasks/questions for the pupils to consider, which are colour-coded orange or red to highlight whether they are merit or distinction level. The teacher gives the pupils the option of either stopping at all of the workstations and completing the relevant merit or distinction tasks or choosing one of the workstations and completing all of the tasks if they failed to include this area at all in their essay.

The tweak

Set up workstations in your room when planning a follow-up feedback lesson.

Teachers often share with us the frustration of many pupils not responding to the extensive feedback we provide them. Although we still use homework time as a means of pupils responding to their feedback, we find that allocating time in class to work on the feedback that has been given is the most useful strategy. Too often, we are forced to rush through realms of content but if pupils are to make steady learning gains, then they will need to be provided with enough time to reflect on areas for improvement and be pointed in the right direction with regards to tasks and resources that will help them close the gap.

Setting up workstations, as in this example, is an excellent strategy that teachers can use when they need to plan a follow-up lesson for feedback. Everyone will be at different points and will have received individual feedback and the teacher needs to have the expert knowledge and skill to set up the workstations to provide appropriate support. Challenge is provided through the teacher encouraging the pupils to decide how they will get the best out of the workstations. Pupils can either focus on the next level up and complete all of the tasks/questions at all of the workstations or, if the essay meets most of the criteria but has missed an essential area, they can concentrate on one area that needs thorough development.

Another useful way to incorporate workstations into your lessons is when pupils have been given differentiated homework activities. Pupils go to the workstation to carry out further work after their initial homework and feedback from the teacher.

Lesson snippet 3

Lesson context: Year 8 Religious education, mixed ability class

Pupils are beginning their topic on religious festivals. On the board is a list of festivals that they can select to research and create a short video on to show the class. They will have three lessons (equivalent to three hours) to make this video. Next to each festival are numbers; these numbers are linked to numbered resources that have been placed around the room. Resources include: newspaper articles; QR codes linked to websites; textbooks; tokens to ask the teacher a question; posters; biographies of religious figures. Pupils decide which religious festival they will research and have ten minutes to scan the relevant resources for their festival. They are then only allowed to have one resource in their possession and the teacher sets a ten-minute timer. After the ten minutes, the pupils can choose another resource and are given a further ten-minute timer. Once pupils have used two resources, they are then given ten minutes to talk to anyone else in the class who has chosen the same festival to research before they must begin planning their video content.

The tweak

Teach pupils how to access and select appropriate resources when working independently of the teacher.

This lesson has the potential to spiral out of control with pupils fighting over resources or not really getting started and messing around instead. The teacher has structured the lesson tightly with regards to timings and instructions to balance the freedom the pupils have been given to choose their content, resources and outcome. For example, the pupils can only have one resource at a time and must use it wisely before handing it back. Another effective strategy is the teacher numbering the resources to stop pupils wasting time finding the ones they think are most useful – the teacher has made a judgement call that this would be too time-consuming for this Year 8 class and could jeopardise the final outcome of informative videos.

This lesson provides a lot of challenge because the pupils can only rely on themselves to ensure they make an informative video. They need to manage their time effectively, be discerning in which resources they choose to use, as well as ask relevant questions to their peers to gain more information from them.

In essence, this lesson has many of the ingredients of project-based learning. If you are going to attempt this style of teaching, then it is important to plan the resources and timings well in advance to ensure it is a success.

Developing independence

The title of this strand is deliberate: developing independence is not to be confused with independent learning. Over the years, there has been much written about the need for more pupils to work independently and to develop their independent learning skills. Indeed, we can't think of many teachers who wouldn't want their pupils to be able to work independently but it is not easy. You can't devote a lesson once a fortnight to working independently; if you do, the quality of the pupils' learning will run the risk of being rather shallow. If you want pupils to develop their independence, it takes time, careful planning and excellent modelling.

Lesson snippet 1

Lesson context: Year 10 Geography, mixed ability class

The teacher sets up a 'Would you rather?' thinking task. The pupils are considering the following scenario: 'You are a poor woman with no formal education, with two children under four. Would you have a better quality of life if you lived in the Philippines or Romania?' The teacher then asks the pupils: 'What information do you need to know to respond to this question?' The teacher sets a timer of eight minutes for the pupils to come up with a 60 second response. After the pupils have written their 60 second response, they then pair up and read their responses to each other. In pairs, they then redraft their response, taking into consideration ideas from both initial responses. The teacher then asks the pairs to move to the left of the room if they think the Philippines, or to the right of the room if they think Romania. The teacher invites targeted pupils to share their responses with the whole class. At the end, pupils are allowed to move if they have changed their minds after hearing different points of view.

The tweak

Using a continuum line to develop independent thinking.

A task in which pupils begin with a view and have time to listen to other ideas before making their decision is a really effective way of helping pupils to think independently. It isn't resource-heavy, yet the pupils have a good opportunity to apply knowledge, state a position in an argument and refine their thinking based on other pupils' responses.

This task makes good use of 'think, pair, share' when pupils read their initial response to their peer before working together to construct a better response, taking the best ideas from both initial responses. Asking pupils to stand in a specific part of the classroom makes it clearly visible to the teacher what her pupils are thinking as well as how their ideas are being refined by their movements around the classroom. However you set up an activity to develop pupils' thinking, try and build in enough time for them to refine their ideas if they don't have enough time to reflect, then the discussion has limited value.

Lesson snippet 2

Lesson context: Year 9 History, mixed ability class

Pupils have been studying the topic, 'slavery', and are now ready to begin their independent learning enquiry. The teacher has posed the question: 'In what ways has the concept of slavery changed from the 18th century?' Pupils must respond to this question in whatever format they choose, focusing on any aspects of slavery they have covered during the topic. The teacher models on the board, using a mind map, the possible routes they might take when responding to the question. After the teacher has modelled possible routes, the pupils begin planning their own enquiry. Once pupils have planned their mind maps, they pin them up around the room. The teacher checks these plans whilst the pupils are given time on the iPads or to look through their exercise books to collate key information they will need for their enquiry. The pupils return to their mind maps on the wall where the teacher has left Post-it notes with questions for the pupils to consider when carrying out their enquiry.

The tweak

Get pupils to plan detailed learning maps before working on an independent project.

Give pupils the opportunity to shape their own learning through the task design. This lesson highlights how taking a risk once the pupils have a secure foundation of knowledge can work well. The teacher is interested in finding out how his pupils have responded to the topic and is now looking for them to apply their knowledge, acknowledging different social and historical contexts. The enquiry question is sufficiently open-ended, which should lead to a range of interesting and original responses. For example, pupils may focus on a particular country's history of slavery whilst some other pupils might focus on the role women play in 18th century and modern day slavery through trafficking.

Make no mistake, this lesson is quite risky because the teacher is letting go and keeping their fingers crossed that the pupils will produce something of quality. However, the teacher has two key moments of input to increase the chance of this lesson being a success; first, he models how to produce a mind map so all pupils have a clear idea of how they can plan their ideas, and then he gives the feedback on their mind maps, posing questions if he feels they may need to develop an idea further. By the time the pupils are ready to produce their enquiry, they should have a very clear and detailed plan to follow.

In any sequence of lessons where the pupils are taking the lead, a structure needs to be provided by the teacher to support the pupils in managing their time. In this case it is a mind map, but learning diaries or timetables are equally useful. Whatever the template, make sure the pupils identify the resources they need, the timings for each mini activity, the desired outcome and their learning intention for their independent project.

Lesson snippet 3

Lesson context: Year 10 Spanish, high ability class

The teacher gives her pupils a blank grid and tells them they need to create an A* marking grid for the topic they have just come to the end of: 'school and future careers'. After 15 minutes, pupils then get into groups of four and compare marking grids; five minutes is given to make any amendments. Once pupils have completed their grids, the teacher displays on the board the subheadings of the generic mark scheme: content; range of language (tenses, sentence structures, vocabulary) and accuracy. Pupils are then given a further couple of minutes to check their marking grid to ensure they have covered all of the criteria. The teacher then shares her version of a top-band marking grid and asks pupils to compare their version with her exemplar. Pupils are told they will be using their marking grid as a learning scaffold when they practise writing about school and future careers next lesson.

The tweak

Create a topic-specific mark scheme using a generic mark scheme to identify how well pupils understand the success criteria.

Understanding the mark scheme is key if a pupil is to be able to work independently. Often, mark schemes can seem impenetrable so setting aside lesson time to make sure pupils have a solid understanding of what is required of them is vital.

In the example above, the teacher wants to test how much knowledge her pupils have retained about the topic they have been working on in order to establish whether they can write an extended piece for a practice assessment. As this is a top set languages class, the teacher hones in on the A* grade criteria, since many of her pupils are working a grade below this in previous writing assessments. Asking pupils to create a topic-specific marking grid is a challenging task; to complete it successfully, pupils will need to remember the different areas of the mark scheme and then consider which topic-specific content and language are more sophisticated than others. The decision to not give any prompts at all at the beginning of the lesson makes this task even more challenging; it is only once the pupils have made an attempt and shared with their peers that the teacher pauses and displays the generic subheadings. Finally, when the teacher shares her exemplar marking grid, this helps the pupils to make a judgement on their own knowledge and what they need to revise before they sit their practice writing assessment in the next lesson.

This activity could be easily adapted for a lower ability group by deciding to have an extended period of teacher modelling or showing a generally good example but deliberately including some aspects of the mark scheme that are inaccurate for the pupils to identify through group discussion.

Category archives: Teaching sequence
David Didau (learningspy.co.uk)

The creative timeline
Pete Jones (deeplearning.edublogs.org) 24 February 2013.

Encouraging independent working – Foldables
Rachel Jones (createinnovateexplore.com) 12 February 2014.

Collaborative learning

In a similar vein to independent learning, collaborative learning – or group work – has been an educational buzzword for a long time. In previous incarnations of the Ofsted framework, teachers were pretty much told they had to include group work if they wanted to be thought of as outstanding. Thankfully, those days are now gone and teachers have a lot more freedom to teach in whatever style they prefer. Nevertheless, we still think that collaborative learning has merit – if carried out effectively. The Education Endowment Foundation toolkit states that collaborative learning has a positive learning gain of five months and ranks highly on their interventions (2014). Therefore, when planning opportunities for collaborative learning, we need to decide why working collaboratively will have a greater impact on learning than pupils working by themselves. In essence, for collaborative learning to be useful, there needs to be a positive cognitive as well as social impact on learning. Finally, sitting them next to each other around a table doesn't necessarily mean pupils are working collaboratively. They need to be taught how to work collaboratively with clear guidelines and learning outcomes.

Google Drive for teachers with 'How-to'
Daniel Edwards (dedwards.me) video links. 16 May 2013.

Top ten group work strategies
Alex Quigley (huntingenglish.com) 12 January 2013.

Collaborative learning – Dylan Wiliam
Dylan Wiliam (journeytoexcellence.org.uk)

Lesson snippet 1

Lesson context: Year 12 BTEC Sport, mixed ability class

Pupils are working on fitness programmes for different athletes. Pupils are working in pairs and are allocated an athlete by the teacher. They have access to the internet to decide on an appropriate fitness programme for their athlete. One pupil is responsible for researching the information and the other pupil is creating the fitness programme using Google Slides, which is the presentation tool on Google Drive. The link for the Google Slides is shared with all of the pupils in the class and their access is set so that they are able to view and edit any slide. After pupils have created their slides for their specific fitness programme, the teacher matches up pairs to give feedback to each other. The pupils are given fifteen minutes to look through the other slides and make changes to their peers' work. At the same time, the teacher is leaving comments for the pupils directly on the slides. At different points in the lesson, the teacher asks pupils to go to a particular slide so that they can critique it as a whole class.

The tweak

Use Google Drive with pupils to make collaboration easy and effective.

Getting pupils to use Google Drive with its shared documents function is an easy way to improve pupils' collaboration. Once every pupil has signed up for Google Drive, they can access each other's work by clicking on the link. Everything is saved in the cloud so there is no need to worry about multiple copies of documents or saving different pupils' work onto a USB stick. Furthermore, Google Drive allows many pupils to work on the same document in real time; there is no annoying 'Read only' message that you get with MS Office if someone else has a document open.

In this lesson, using Google Slides (Google's version of PowerPoint) helps the pupils to collaborate effectively; they can instantly give feedback to their peers or read other pupils' work to see if their programme is appropriate for the athlete. The teacher can monitor the slides from his own computer and give helpful pointers during the lesson.

For those teachers who want to make the most of online learning tools to enhance pupils' learning, then Google classroom could be the answer. Google classroom is a free online space for teachers to set up virtual classrooms; in the virtual classroom, the teacher and pupils have access to all of the Google drive tools when creating work. All work is uploaded to Google classroom and pupils can see each other's work and comments left by the teacher and other pupils. The teacher has the option of posting an assignment and pupils can share an announcement with their peers and attach files from Google drive, a YouTube video or a website link.

Lesson snippet 2

Lesson context: Year 10 Maths, middle ability class

Pupils are coming to the end of the topic, 'probability'. The teacher informs the pupils that they will need to create a ten-question test for their partner on the topic. They need to create the ten questions and provide an answer sheet which details their workings out. Pupils are not allowed to use their textbooks; the aim is to see how much the pupils have retained from their previous lessons. The pupils begin to create their ten-question test and the accompanying answer sheet with their workings out. The teacher pairs up the pupils and they begin to answer the test questions. After 15 minutes, the teacher stops the pupils and the pupils mark each other's tests. Where there are gaps because the pupils do not remember how to work something out or where the pupils have got a question incorrect, the other pupil shares their answer sheets. The pupils then feedback to the teacher how many answers their peer got correct and what they think their peer still needs to work on before the end of topic test.

The tweak

Pupils become test buddies to support each other's learning.

Getting pupils to plan resources for tasks to use collaboratively is a really effective way for teachers to identify how much pupils have remembered. The teacher is very clear that the pupils are not allowed to use any resources; this is a middle ability class and she is using her professional judgement in deciding how much she wants to challenge her pupils. It is fairly easy for a pupil to make a test paper for another peer; what increases the challenge of this task is that pupils have to provide a very specific type of answer sheet where they show all of the steps of their workings out. This is a very useful resource for their partner because they can make use of it if they get stuck. By breaking down the workings out, the pupils can easily identify at what point they began to go wrong. Another effective addition to the lesson is the teacher asking for feedback from the pupils. She will know from the amount of questions that are answered correctly as well as the areas that the pupils think their partners needs to revise how to adapt her planning to ensure they are ready for the end of topic test. Pupils making resources for each other is a good way to see the learning from the pupils' perspective. It gives us an insight into how pupils think they learn best – an important strand of metacognition and not to be confused with visual, auditory and kinaesthetic learning styles (VAK)!

Lesson snippet 3

Lesson context: Year 11 Chemistry, high ability class

The teacher has set up his room as a marketplace where the tables now become a stall. At each stall, there are seven pupils who are responsible for informing other pupils about specific information relating to the topic 'oils'. The pupils have been given a choice about how they present their information: a video made using the iPad app 'Explain Everything', a selection of annotated diagrams or a 3D model. Each pupil will have a visitor come to their stall for three minutes where the visitor needs to glean as much information as possible before they move on. The teacher decides which pupils visit which stalls. The teacher sets the timer; pupils begin moving to the different stalls and take notes as they go. After three minutes, each visitor is allowed a further two minutes to ask the stallholder a question before moving on. Once the pupils have visited all of their assigned stalls, they return to their original seat and collate their notes in preparation for doing a past exam paper.

The tweak

Set up a marketplace in your classroom where pupils learn from each other.

Using a marketplace format works well when the teacher has just marked pupils' work and has a good grasp of their strengths and areas for improvement. The teacher then sets homework for pupils to produce either the video, annotated diagrams or a 3D model based on their strengths – that way, the teacher knows they will be able to produce something useful for other pupils who find a particular aspect of the topic difficult. As well as this, the pupils should appreciate being given choice with regards to what they produce for their peers.

During the lesson, the teacher has used pupil data to decide who is going to benefit from visiting the different stalls based on their performance in the previous practice exam paper. Pupils are able to pick up the information they are lacking at present, make notes and then feel more confident before they attempt another paper. Also, the teacher has built in time to allow pupils to ask questions to the stallholders if they need something explained or a misconception clarified. The marketplace format means the teacher is able to take a step back, gauge the temperature of the class and reflect on whether the pupils are closing their knowledge gaps and are better prepared for the next practice paper.

Another effective way a marketplace can be used is when pupils have been given different homework or revision topics and pupils share what they have learnt. Afterwards, pupils can be given an activity where they need to include a certain amount of information they have learnt from visiting the different marketplace stalls.

Annotated Business studies lesson plan

Teacher	Date and period	Subject	Class and ability range	Boy:girl ratio
Miss Lunn	2/04/P1	GCSE Business studies	Year 10 mixed ability	13:12

	Student context:	EAL	SEN	G&T
		8	7	1

Learning objective	Differentiated learning outcomes
To understand the assessment objectives required to be successful in the coursework.	1. Identify connectives for analysis (AO3) and examples of application (AO2). 2. Identify and understand evaluative writing (AO3). 3. Use AO1/2/3 in their essay writing focus task.

Resources needed
PowerPoint, highlighters, hook/plenary Facebook update sheet, writing frame, A grade answer, challenge sheet, support glossary, research.

Lesson content	Planned opportunities to check prior knowledge and further pupil progress
Hook What do you already know about essay writing? Complete first Facebook update.	Self-assessment of what you already know about essay writing.
New learning activities Introduce the coursework (Unit 2). Recall of assessment objectives (AOs). Demonstration of essay writing structure. ← Read A grade essay. In groups identify examples of AO1/AO2/AO3 (each group member looking for a different AO). ←	Each group gives feedback. Exam board criteria are used throughout the lesson. Pupils have previously written their own versions of the criteria under the official ones to ensure they are fully accessible.
Pit stop (Reflection activity) What do they mean?– match up activity of terminology used in AOs.	
New learning activity Individual task – using the writing frame complete the 'mini essay' focus task using knowledge of AOs.	Writing frame – to maximise marks. Teacher feedback – giving and receiving feedback according to assessment criteria.
Plenary (Reflection activity) What do you now know about essay writing? – complete Facebook update.	Plenary checking understanding of assessment objectives through Facebook update.

Using an exemplar piece of work to model how an essay can be structured means pupils have a meaningful picture of what they are aiming for.

Making each pupil responsible for a different aspect (AO) makes this is a truly collaborative task because every person in the group is needed to complete the whole task.

Questions have been carefully planned for specific pupils based upon their ability. The teacher uses follow-up questions in many cases to further challenge each pupil.

Teacher plans to spend time with target groups each lesson to ensure all pupils have a regular input of focused teacher support and challenge.

Differentiation strategies used in the lesson	Through task	Through questioning all stages	Through groupings	Through teacher and other adults' support
S – Starter NL – New learning activity R – Reflection activity T – Throughout	R - Writing frame Teacher/peer support. R – Additional research source for more able. NL – support glossary for lowest ability/SEN pupils.	Self-assessment, peer and teacher questioning. Questions planned at different levels of challenge to be targeted to the appropriate pupils.	Mixed-ability groups.	Teacher support and checking where needed. Teacher to focus on more able pupils.

Support resources are available for pupils to take if they need them. Although they are sometimes used, just knowing that they are available if needed encourages pupils to challenge themselves and make a start without them.

Literacy/numeracy links
Practise using connectives – highlighting AO2/3.

Homework task
Your coursework will be based around a business of your choice. Choose a local business to you. Either brainstorm how they use innovation to help their business to be successful or write a questionnaire for their customers to identify whether they think innovation is important for the success of the business. ←

Giving pupils an element of choice can help encourage those who are reluctant to complete homework. The choices could provide options for different levels of challenge or alternatively could encourage pupils to be more creative by considering different ways to present similar information.

Stretch and challenge provision in Business studies lesson plan

- There are well-planned opportunities for independence. There are planned opportunities for dialogue between pupils about the work, which means they support each other's learning. There are also resources available when they are stuck. This means the teacher is available to provide extra support where needed and to ask well-targeted questions.

- Pupils will work in small groups so will have opportunities to consolidate their understanding by talking through their ideas with their peers. This means pupils will be more confident when tackling the challenge of the individual written task.

- The differentiation is more than just by outcome. The teacher has planned specific questions for certain pupils based upon their ability and asks follow up questions when pupils answer correctly.

- There is task differentiation where the brightest pupils are provided with an extension research task to complete and the lower ability pupils are given a support glossary.

- The homework is differentiated to challenge different abilities and prepares pupils for following lessons.

Missed opportunities and tweaks

Missed opportunity

Although the use of an exemplar essay is excellent practice, this is unsuitable for many members of the class. This is a mixed ability GCSE group so reading the A grade essay could be too much for many pupils and could lead to them switching off.

The tweak

It is important to stretch and challenge all your pupils, but remember to consider their starting points. Using a range of exemplar essays (for example at grades A, C and E) and putting pupils into groups of similar ability would be a better way to achieve this. Each group could be given an essay that is slightly above the level they are currently working at or alternatively could be given two essays and asked to look at the differences between them.

Missed opportunity

The group task where pupils identify examples of each assessment objective (AO) needs to be differentiated. The plan is for pupils to select the AO they want to look at, but the AOs become progressively more challenging and this is not taken into consideration.

The tweak

Differentiating a task of looking for a particular aspect (here, the AOs) in an exemplar piece of work could be achieved in different ways. If you put your pupils into mixed ability groups, you could assign a different aspect to each pupil, according to their ability. Alternatively, if pupils are working in groups based on ability, each group could look at an aspect of a different level of challenge or you could provide more or less support as appropriate.

Missed opportunity

During the individual written task, the plan is to automatically give out resources to the G&T and SEN pupils without consideration of whether they are actually needed or how this could affect motivation of these or other pupils in the class.

The tweak

Rather than giving out resources automatically to particular ability groups the decision could be left to the pupils themselves. One of the approaches that you could try is to describe tasks as 'warm', 'hot' or 'scorching' as they become progressively more difficult. The key is that the pupils themselves choose how to make the task sufficiently challenging and you can monitor which level of difficulty a pupil has chosen.

Missed opportunity

The teacher has decided to spend all of her time with the least able pupils during the written task at the end. This may be the best use of her time and she may be planning to focus on this group for this particular lesson. However, some of the more able pupils might struggle with the extension task and start to lose focus.

The tweak

If support resources are available for pupils to use as and when required, it may be that you need to plan to focus your time checking the level of tasks your pupils have chosen and questioning the more able pupils to ensure they are coping with the level of difficulty. This doesn't mean that the less able pupils should just be left to fend for themselves: you could enlist the help of the more able pupils to assist in monitoring the progress of the less able pupils if you feel this will be an appropriate challenge for them.

In summary. . .

It takes careful planning over time to develop an effective and sufficiently challenging learning environment. Giving pupils more choice over how much support they need, will lead to them wanting to challenge themselves. Having the option of support available means pupils are more likely to take risks because they know it is there if they need it.

Annotated PE lesson plan

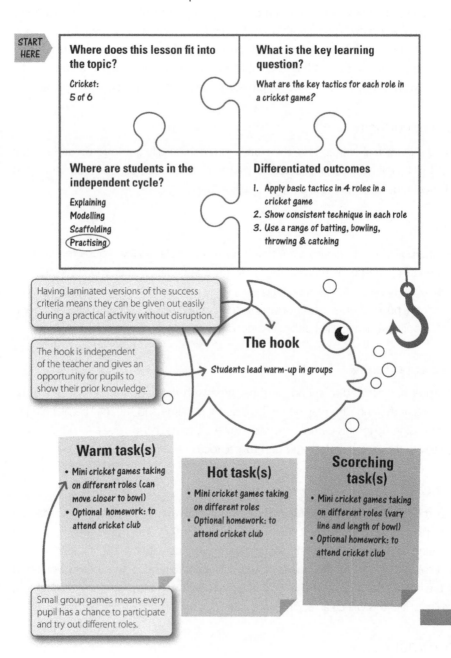

START HERE

Where does this lesson fit into the topic?

Cricket:
5 of 6

What is the key learning question?

What are the key tactics for each role in a cricket game?

Where are students in the independent cycle?

Explaining
Modelling
Scaffolding
Practising

Differentiated outcomes

1. Apply basic tactics in 4 roles in a cricket game
2. Show consistent technique in each role
3. Use a range of batting, bowling, throwing & catching

Having laminated versions of the success criteria means they can be given out easily during a practical activity without disruption.

The hook is independent of the teacher and gives an opportunity for pupils to show their prior knowledge.

The hook

Students lead warm-up in groups

Warm task(s)

- Mini cricket games taking on different roles (can move closer to bowl)
- Optional homework: to attend cricket club

Hot task(s)

- Mini cricket games taking on different roles
- Optional homework: to attend cricket club

Scorching task(s)

- Mini cricket games taking on different roles (vary line and length of bowl)
- Optional homework: to attend cricket club

Small group games means every pupil has a chance to participate and try out different roles.

Monitoring progress points

1. T observes group warm up

2. T questions umpires on the rules

3. T observes each role in each group

4. Peer feedback, observed by T

As the pupils evaluate each other's performance, the teacher listens to their conversations helping her to assess how well pupils understand each role.

Groupings

Individual
- N/A

Pair
- Peer assessment discussions

Group
- Ability groups of 3 for warm up
- Ability groups of 6 for cricket games

The teacher has invested time to train the class to move between groups quickly, which frees her up to observe and question the pupils.

Key words

Bowl
Bat
Wicket
Field
Outfield
Catch
Umpire
Spin
Swing

Ask before pupils are given success criteria to encourage independent thinking.

Questions to develop thinking

Which skills are you using in your role?

The takeaway

What do you think is the most important tactic in each of the 4 roles in a cricket game?

Stretch and challenge provision in PE lesson plan

- The lesson plan begins with the pupils leading the warm-up. Every pupil will participate because they each decide on one exercise for the warm-up. It is evident that the teacher has trained her pupils to work independently in this way and it frees up the teacher to ask challenging questions.

- Pupils will come up with their own success criteria for each of the roles that the teacher has introduced. Only after this has been discussed will the pupils be given the level criteria so they can compare their ideas to the different levels. This challenges pupils to consider what is expected of them throughout the lesson and will make them more confident when evaluating their performance.

- As the pupils evaluate each other's performance, the teacher will listen to these conversations to assess how well the pupils understand each role. The teacher plans to pick out some good examples from these conversations to share at the end.

Missed opportunities and tweaks

Missed opportunity

The teacher plans to put the pupils into mixed-ability groups and ask the pupils to support each other. The outcome in such situations is often that in some groups the stronger pupils dominate in the physical task whilst the weaker pupils are intimidated; whereas in other groups, the more able pupils are obviously held back and become frustrated. This does not achieve the stretch and challenge for all pupils.

The tweak

The tweak is pretty straightforward: group the pupils according to ability. Then you can adapt tasks slightly for different groups and pupils of similar ability can learn from each other. It also means that you can work with pupils at a particular level if appropriate.

Missed opportunity

The grouping can also cause some problems with the peer evaluation conversations as very able pupils will be discussing techniques with much lower ability pupils. The pupils are working at very different levels, so the less able pupils may struggle to give effective feedback to their more able partner.

The tweak

In many cases, particularly here in the cricket game, grouping pupils by ability means skills of an appropriate level can be practised, so pupils can be stretched and not held back by their peers. You can use pupils who demonstrate good skills within a specific role or area to model those skills to the rest of their group, to help pupils focus on moving up to the next level.

In summary. . .

There is a place for mixed ability grouping and using higher ability pupils to support the less able; however, for many tasks involving group work it is best to group by ability. This will ensure you can effectively support and still sufficiently stretch and challenge every pupil.

Top tweaks checklist: stretch and challenge

- Challenge pupils by making them compare their work with that from a pupil who is one level/grade higher but no more; otherwise seeing work that is so much better than yours is intimidating and often seems out of reach.
- Differentiate a task where pupils are working in mixed ability groups by assigning different things to focus on.
- Refrain from handing out resources automatically to particular ability groups of pupils because this stops them from challenging themselves. One of the approaches that could be used is to describe tasks as 'warm', 'hot' or 'scorching' as they become progressively more difficult.
- Ask more able pupils to support less able pupils by checking on their progress once they have finished their work. These pupils can become 'teachers' by offering advice and support to ensure the less able pupils can access the task.
- Plan in advance the questions you want to ask your pupils using Bloom's taxonomy to ensure pupils are being challenged further by having to respond to higher level questions.
- Accept that it will take time for pupils to feel comfortable and confident asking each other questions – it won't happen overnight. You will need to support them in developing these questioning skills by creating resources such as question stems, Bloom's pyramid or basic fill-in-the blank frames.
- Make extension tasks available to all pupils but set conditions that need to be fulfilled before pupils are given the task so you can ensure they complete and understand the core tasks first; if you raise your expectations, your pupils will do the same.

Learning leader: stretch and challenge

- Use the zones of learning target in training with staff (see online resources and appendix 2). Ask staff how they would identify pupils in each zone, what questions they would ask pupils in each zone or strategies they would use to get their pupils out of the panic or comfort zones and into the stretch zone. Staff may also wish to discuss how they could use the target in lessons with their pupils to encourage them to challenge themselves further.

- It is important to plan the most effective grouping strategy for particular tasks; both in terms of group size and ability composition. Spend some time as a department discussing firstly the types of tasks pupils are assigned in your subject and secondly how best pupils should be grouped. For example, in science it may be the case that practical work can be completed in a mixed ability group because practical skills do not necessarily correlate with academic level but a task that requires pupils to collaborate on a written report will need to be completed in similar ability pairs.

- The following activity could be used in a mixed training setting or in a departmental training session. Ask staff to bring a range of tasks that they have used with their classes over the past week. Staff can work individually or in pairs to look at the tasks and discuss how they could be tweaked to make them warm, hot or scorching. The idea is that it isn't always necessary to spend hours planning separate tasks for different levels of challenge – a bank of simple tweaks could be created to be used regularly in lessons. For example, a written task could be converted from hot to scorching by specifying a particular audience, such as a group of designers, or by limiting the length of the piece to 50 words or fewer. Similarly, a task could be made warm by allowing pupils to use a text book or by letting pupils work in a pair.

- One of the problems that can arise when giving pupils a choice of the level of a task is that they select an inappropriate level. This can be a concern, as the whole point of this approach is to give pupils more control over their level by offering them the choice. In a training session, to encourage staff to plan for such situations, give them scenarios of pupils selecting inappropriate levels of work and discuss what to do. This could be done through role play, but if you cringe at the prospect, you could instead write the scenarios on large pieces of paper, ask staff to add some responses on sticky notes and then discuss the different ideas.

- Suggested staff enquiry questions for stretch and challenge could include: 'Which grouping strategies are most effective to challenge pupils for the main types of activity I use with my Year 9 classes?' or 'How can I introduce task choice to pupils whilst ensuring the level of challenge is appropriate for every pupil?'

5 Commitment to learning

(Not to be confused with leaving them to get on with it so you can get some marking done...)

Many educational experts have highlighted the importance of developing independent learners rather than just spoon feeding pupils to pass examinations. There can be no doubt that this benefits the pupil: both in terms of academic success and employability. It is also beneficial to the teacher as they can use the opportunity to spend more valuable time with each pupil and carefully target their intervention and questioning.

In order to develop independence in our learners, we need to step back and give our pupils opportunities to take control of their own learning and make decisions for themselves. Lessons need to be planned carefully to develop group work skills and provide extended tasks over a lesson or series of lessons.

The presentation of these tasks also needs to be considered. If you are going to leave your pupils to 'get on with it' you will need to feel confident that the pupils won't lose their focus and just use the freedom to have a bit of a chat. Some pupils will simply get on because they are motivated and independent already, some will enjoy having more ownership of tasks and may just need guidance from time to time whilst others will need more of an incentive. It may be helpful to inject some competition into tasks using a points system that the pupils could design themselves, however, sometimes just having a clear audience and purpose for a piece of work will provide the necessary motivation for pupils to produce their best work. In *An ethic of excellence* (Berger, 2003), Ron Berger discusses the importance of changing the culture in the classroom to one that accepts nothing less than excellent work. 'If you're going to do something, I believe, you should do it well. You should sweat over it and make sure it's strong and accurate and beautiful and you should be proud of it.'

Dealing with getting stuck

How many times have you heard one of your pupils say, 'I can't do this. It's too hard!' in a wheedling voice? The issue we have is that most pupils don't like getting stuck. They don't want to look stupid in front of their peers, so they either won't attempt new learning in case they can't do it or they will have a go and then blame you when they can't do it first time.

One option is to reduce the challenge but that smacks of low teacher expectations; instead, we need to invest time in establishing a safe learning environment where risks are taken and nobody is ridiculed for getting it wrong. It's a culture where pupils are rewarded for their effort and commitment rather than being overly praised for getting things right without struggling. This last point is a timely one because it seems to go against what we instinctively believe; surely pupils should be praised if they do something well. Unfortunately, it's not as simple as this. Professor Rob Coe's research report 'What makes great teaching?' highlights that lavish praise actually has a negative impact on pupils' learning and progress because it is a sign of teachers having low expectations and capping what they think a pupil's potential is (Coe et. al., 2014). It is important to distinguish between pupils doing what you expect of them and pupils doing something that exceeds your expectations.

Lesson snippet 1

Lesson context: Year 13 Sociology, mixed ability class

Pupils are preparing for their exam topic, 'mass media'. The teacher displays an exam question on the board: 'To what extent do sociological arguments and evidence support the view that the representation of ethnic minorities in the mass media is problematic and often negative?' Pupils are told that they have five minutes to plan their ideas and that they are not allowed to talk during this time. They are then asked to look at their plans and consider the weakest points. Once they have identified their weakest points, the teacher gives them three options: a stuck card, a critical friend and a timeout. The stuck card can be used to clarify a sociological argument with the teacher; they can only ask one question. A critical friend can be used to ask another pupil to read part of the essay and critique it. A timeout can be used to leave the table and look something up in their notes or the textbook. The teacher explains to the pupils that these options offer different types of support: do they need clarification, support with developing their writing style or time to increase their factual knowledge? All pupils can only use one of the support options and must state which one they want before they begin writing.

The tweak

Train pupils to be discerning in how they use different types of support.

The structure of this lesson is really effective in encouraging pupils to work out for themselves what their weaknesses are and what support they think will be most useful. It would have been easy for the teacher to offer all three types of support to her pupils but too much support when writing an essay could lead to a poor indication of what the pupil will be capable of in the real exam. There is no support in the exam so the teacher is trying to get her pupils into a position where they can answer practice papers under exam conditions. These pupils are becoming resilient because they have to decide on the level of support before they begin writing; they can't change their minds halfway through so it should make them consider much more carefully their own learning needs.

Lesson snippet 2

Lesson context: Year 8 English, middle ability class

Pupils have been reading *The boy in the striped pyjamas* and the teacher has introduced extracts of non-fiction from World War II. The task is for pupils to create their own non-fiction text, either a letter from a soldier or a piece of propaganda, based on something they have read in the novel. Pupils have previously struggled with writing non-fiction texts so the teacher has on display a 'learning zone diagram'. The teacher asks the question: 'Which zone are you in – panic, stretch or comfort?' Pupils write their name on a Post-it note and place it in the zone which best describes them. The teacher selects a pupil from each zone and asks them to expand upon why they have put their Post-it there. The teacher listens to a selection of the pupils sharing their concerns about non-fiction writing; the teacher, from listening to the pupils' comments, recognises that the pupils have a greater levels of confidence when writing fiction texts. The teacher ends the class discussion by asking pupils to work in pairs to come up with two things they could do this lesson to stretch themselves and take a risk with their work. She also makes clear that she will not allow any questions for the first ten minutes to allow enough time for the pupils to make a start with their writing.

The tweak

Give pupils time and space to come up with their own solutions to problems they encounter.

It is important to create an environment where pupils feel confident to articulate how they are feeling. If a pupil feels panicked about tackling something challenging, then there are two likely reactions: pupils either refuse to even try or they have a go but quickly get upset. If a pupil is in the comfort zone then they may not try their best, thinking the work is too easy for them. You want pupils to be in the stretch zone, where they are finding something difficult but have a plan about how they can engage with the task. The key is to help pupils recognise what zone they're in and if it's not the stretch zone, what needs to happen to get them there. In this lesson, the teacher asks the pupils to work in pairs to decide how they can take responsibility for ensuring they are in the stretch zone. They have to think carefully about the difficulties they might face with the task and consider possible strategies to overcome their difficulties to produce a good-quality piece of work.

Lesson snippet 3

Lesson context: Year 10 Computing, high ability class

Pupils are halfway through their programming controlled assessment and the teacher displays the marking criteria on the board. Many of the pupils are reaching a point where they are finding the work really challenging. The teacher uses the start of the lesson as a checkpoint to monitor how the pupils are progressing with the controlled assessment. He asks them to identify where precisely they began to get stuck and write it on the board. The teacher begins to troubleshoot using the following three questions: 'What knowledge do you need to get to the next stage of your programming?' 'What do you know how to do confidently?' 'How are you going to find out how to do the thing you can't do presently?' Pupils write their responses down and the teacher collects their feedback. He then displays hyperlinks to several YouTube videos which show viewers how to do different aspects of programming using Java. The teacher tells his pupils that they must use these videos to overcome the difficulties they are experiencing.

The tweak

Ask pupils to question themselves about why they're stuck before selecting appropriate resources to get unstuck.

When pupils are working towards a long-term goal such as completing a controlled assessment, they can begin with good intentions but lose some of their initial optimism when they start facing difficulties. The easy way out would be to spoon feed the pupils and just tell them how to do it – but that's not helping them to become better learners. Inevitably, they will face more problems later in the course and their first thought will be that they don't need to try because the teacher will do it for them. To help pupils overcome these difficulties, teachers need to have a structured approach to troubleshooting. If you ask the right questions, then you get helpful feedback from the pupils and you can begin to point them in the right direction in terms of receiving appropriate resources to move them forward. In this case, the teacher does not tell the pupils which videos they should watch; there is a fairly long list and it is up to the pupils to work out for themselves which ones will be most relevant for them.

Sowing seeds in September
Shaun Allison (classteaching.wordpress.com) 19 August 2014.

TM Clevedon workshop: Engagement & courageous curiosity
Zoë Elder (fullonlearning.com) 15 June 2013.

Developing olympic learners
David Fawcett (reflectionsofmyteaching.blogspot.co.uk) 7 October 2012.

Growth mindset

Growth mindset is a culture that we can foster in our pupils by making them recognise the relationship between effort and achievement. If a pupil has a growth mindset then they believe that they can get better at something if they work hard. Unfortunately, we know that sometimes even the most hardworking of pupils don't always get what they deserve. We need to be realistic with our pupils about this fact; yet we also need to instil in them that success is linked to the effort you put in and that intelligence is not fixed. At the heart of it all is the language we use in the classroom. The more we make explicit the highs and lows of learning, the more likely our pupils will become confident and capable learners.

Lesson snippet 1

Lesson context: Year 10 BTEC Business studies, mixed ability class
The final BTEC Business lesson of the week is always set aside for pupils to reflect on their progress during the unit of study. The pupils are working on brand development and are studying different ways to maximise brand potential. The teacher has set up a whole class blog; the blog is used by the pupils to keep track of what they are learning and to review feedback on their work from their peers and the teacher. There are also links to pupils' e-portfolios where they store their work. Pupils blog at the end of each week about what they had hoped to achieve at the beginning of the week, problems they encountered during the lessons and aspects of their work this week that they think is worthy of praise. The teacher has allocated a 'critical friend' to each pupil whose responsibility it is to leave feedback for their peer. After they have given feedback, the teacher then shares their feedback, commenting on what they saw and heard in class with suggestions for the following week's lessons.

The tweak

Set up a blog for pupils to comment on their learning over time.

Setting up a class blog is an excellent way to engage pupils in the process of reviewing their work. There are two key strengths to this blog. First, the pupils are taking responsibility for its upkeep; they know that they will not receive written feedback from their teacher unless they take time to share their successes and problems. Secondly, pupils are also responsible for each other's learning when they write up their feedback on the blog. Again, the teacher makes it clear that pupils will not receive any teacher feedback for the week if they do not fulfil their responsibility as 'critical friend' to their peer. The blog works as an essential strategy for the teacher to establish a classroom culture of acknowledging the process of learning as well as the final outcome. Learning is difficult and the blog works as a reminder to pupils of how they must overcome difficulties if they are to meet their teacher's high expectations.

Lesson snippet 2

Lesson context: Year 11 Physics, high ability class

Pupils are reviewing their learning after completing their first controlled assessment before they attempt their second controlled assessment. The teacher shares with the pupils that the aim of the lesson is to consider where they made mistakes during the three parts of the controlled assessment – planning, observations and conclusions – and how they managed to learn from their mistakes and move forward with their investigation. Pupils are asked to move to the 'FAIL then SAIL' display board. FAIL stands for 'First Attempt In Learning' and SAIL stands for 'Second Attempt in Learning'. Pupils are given a few minutes to think about moments when they made mistakes the first time they attempted new things during the investigation. They then share these moments with other pupils on their table. Then the teacher asks them to think about moments when they showed improvements when they attempted tasks where they had previously made mistakes. The teacher asks pupils to think about why they were able to make fewer errors the second time around; what did they learn that helped them to produce better planning, observations and conclusions? Pupils then share their second attempts in learning. Each pupil is asked to select one key FAIL and SAIL moment and pin them on the board to share with the class.

The tweak

Create a board where pupils can visibly track how they learn from their mistakes.

The concept of growth mindset, introduced by Carol Dweck, concentrates on the idea that pupils recognise that their abilities are not fixed; it teaches pupils to not only accept failure as part of the learning experience but to actively embrace it if they want to become better learners: 'no matter what your ability is, effort is what ignites that ability and turns it into accomplishment'. (Dweck, 2006). This teacher uses the acronyms of FAIL and SAIL after seeing them used on Twitter and has made the decision to introduce his top set class to the concept of accepting and embracing failure. This FAIL and SAIL display board is used routinely by the pupils when they review their learning. Many teachers of top sets find that one of the problems they face is that pupils who are used to being labelled as successful, find it difficult to cope when things go wrong. Finding a common language for talking about moments of failure and how to overcome them with your pupils is really important; once pupils begin to take risks, knowing that failure is not the end of the world, their knowledge, skills and understanding become far more developed and sophisticated.

Lesson snippet 3

Lesson context: Year 7 Maths, low ability class

Pupils are preparing for a test on two topics that they have been studying over the past six weeks. The teacher asks them to think about the three things they have found most difficult. Pupils are given time to discuss their difficulties with their peers. The teacher then hands out an action plan template (see online resources and appendix 3) to use to create a structured approach to improving their knowledge. Before the pupils complete their action plans, the teacher models to the class something that she finds difficult using the action plan template. The questions she asks herself aloud as she completes the action plan are: 'What do I find difficult?' 'How do I react when I find things difficult?' 'What have I tried doing already to learn this?' 'What else could I try that I haven't thought of?' 'What specific time slots do I have available which I will make use of to become better?' 'Why is it important that I try and improve in this area?' Pupils then work individually to complete their plans before handing them in to the teacher, who tells them that she will be coming back to the plans over the next fortnight to check that they are taking responsibility for being as prepared as they can for the upcoming test.

The tweak

Pupils produce an improvement action plan as a tool for assessment preparation.

Pupils who are in a low ability class and have not had much experience of success can often be quite defensive and close-minded about what they think they can achieve. We've all heard pupils say, 'I'm rubbish', 'I can't do it' or 'There's no point in me trying because I've never done well before'. In these circumstances, you might need to take a step back from teaching content for a short time and work out how these pupils are feeling about your subject. Just because we love our subjects doesn't necessarily mean that they will! In this example, the teacher has created a simple but structured approach to help the pupils work out that they can make a difference to their learning. The teacher immediately begins to create a safe and trusting environment by modelling to her pupils that she has weaknesses too. She explicitly demonstrates how she reacts to failure but, crucially, also highlights that hard work and sustained effort go a long way to help her improve. By handing in their action plans to the teacher, the pupils are entering into a contract with her that they are going to work hard to try and improve. By stating that she will monitor whether they are doing the things they've said they will, she is showing them that she is taking them seriously and treating them as responsible learners rather than spoon feeding them.

A grand day out with Dweck, Syed, Hymer, Brinton, Jones & Elder
Shaun Allison (classteaching.wordpress.com) 8 July 2014.

Top ten tips for developing a growth mindset in your classroom
Pete Jones (deeplearning.edublogs.org) 3 August 2014.

This much I know about…developing a Dweck-inspired growth mindset culture
John Tomsett (johntomsett.com) 20 October 2013.

Creating a culture of excellence

Committed learners recognise that learning is and should be a struggle. They embrace the challenges they encounter and seek out feedback to improve. In effect, committed learners play their part in creating a learning environment which is defined by a culture of excellence. As mentioned earlier in the chapter (page 91), Ron Berger has had considerable influence on how teachers talk about excellence if they have his book *An ethic of excellence*. When talking to teachers, the perennial concern is the lack of time to cover curriculum content in enough depth which hinders the quest for a culture of excellence. In reality, not every single piece of work a pupil does can be scrutinised with the detail that Berger explores in his book. Nonetheless, it is relatively straightforward to decide in advance which pieces of work will undergo the planning, drafting, editing and refining approach which embodies the spirit of Berger's book.

Creating a culture of critique
David Fawcett (reflectionsofmyteaching.blogspot.co.uk) 6 April 2013.

The butterfly effect
Eliza O'Driscoll (failingbettereverytime.wordpress.com) 21 August 2014.

Defining the butterfly: Knowing the standards to set the standards
Tom Sherrington (headguruteacher.com) 20 November 2013.

Lesson snippet 1

Lesson context: Year 8 Design and technology, mixed ability class

Pupils are working on their textiles project to make a bag. Pupils are at the final stages of design, having spent four lessons developing a range of different designs. They need to make a decision this lesson about what their final design will be before they begin making their bag. They leave their workbooks out for other pupils to look at and comment on; the teacher has given pupils a series of questions to consider when giving feedback: 'Which design do you think is the best and why?' 'Looking at the design you think is best, what makes it better than the others?' 'Is there anything you think your peer should do before moving on to making their bag?' During the peer feedback, the teacher looks at the workbooks too, noting down particular designs that he considers to be examples of excellence. Once the pupils have received their feedback, they are asked to share which design has received the most positive feedback and state whether they agree. The teacher then displays photographs of the four designs he has chosen which he thinks are examples of excellence and asks pupils to consider, using the success criteria, why he has chosen these particular designs.

The tweak

Use success criteria to make explicit to pupils which pieces of work have met the standard of excellence.

Part of creating a culture of excellence is the ability to welcome criticism. There is little value in celebrating efforts that fall short of the high expectations the teacher has set for the pupils. This can be quite daunting for pupils initially. 'What if my work isn't chosen?' 'What if the teacher thinks my work isn't good enough?' These are questions that pupils might ask themselves at the beginning. The only way these anxieties can be overcome is if the teacher is totally committed to creating a culture where effort as opposed to ability is praised. Pupils are not there to compete against each other; rather, they are there to beat their personal best every time they enter the class. Pupils expect to get feedback from their peers and teacher but it is often private. Opening up your work to be scrutinised by your peers and teacher can be uncomfortable. However, making it public allows the teacher to highlight and celebrate excellence, which ultimately encourages pupils to give their best effort at all times.

Lesson snippet 2

Lesson context: Year 9 History, mixed ability class

Pupils are working on writing effective introductions for an essay on the causes of World War I. The teacher leads a class discussion on what they should include in their essay introduction; criteria are formulated, focusing on content and writing style. Then, pupils are given ten minutes to draft their first attempt at an introduction. After ten minutes, pupils read over their paragraph and identify where they have met the criteria. The teacher then puts the pupils into pairs; each pupil shares with their partner what they think their work is lacking based on the success criteria. Pupils verbally offer suggestions about what they might do to improve this particular aspect of the introduction. Pupils are given another ten minutes to write their second attempt at an introduction. Pupils then get back into their pairs and read each other's second draft, commenting on whether it is an improvement on the first. The teacher then chooses two pupils' drafts and uses the visualiser to display them for the class. She asks pupils to consider which draft meets all of the success criteria. After pupils have decided which draft is best, they are then given a further five minutes to make their final edits to their introduction.

The tweak

Set aside time in the topic for whole lessons on drafting and editing before the assessment.

Another important aspect of creating a culture of excellence is for pupils to realise that excellence takes time; it is very rare that a pupil's first attempt will be their best work. Pupils need to get used to the concept of drafting. In our experience pupils really resent drafting their work; it's boring, takes a lot of effort and requires them to scrutinise the smallest details of their work. Some pupils are used to being praised for finishing a piece of work, regardless of whether it has met all aspects of the criteria. The teacher telling pupils that they need to write the same paragraph again and again might meet with cries of 'What? I've written loads already.' However, in this lesson, the teacher has no fancy tricks up her sleeve; there are no gimmicks, just plain hard work – a lot of it happening in silence whilst the pupils write their introductions. If the teacher is to create a culture of excellence and inspire the pupils to want to produce their best, regardless of how difficult or boring that might be, then pupils need to be challenged with, 'It might be finished – but is it good enough yet?' By giving pupils the opportunity to hear suggestions from their peers and see quality examples on the board, they are encouraged to step back from a subjective response to their work and consider if it really is good enough to say, 'I'm finished'.

Lesson snippet 3

Lesson context: Year 12 Economics, mixed ability class

Pupils come to class with their essay on whether profit maximisation is always the most important objective of a business. The teacher splits the class in half; each half of the class, using the exam board mark scheme, must rank the essays produced by the pupils in their group. The teacher allocates 20 minutes for pupils to read the essays in silence and then individually decide on their ranking. After 20 minutes, pupils then share with their group what they think is the correct ranking. The teacher listens to the groups' discussion and poses questions about their essays. Each group pins up their essays in rank order. The teacher takes the highest ranked essay from each group and reads them aloud to the whole class. The teacher confirms that both essays would get an A grade but pupils are asked which would receive the highest mark in the exam. Once pupils have decided which essay is the best in the class, the teacher tells the pupils that they will all – apart from the two A grade answers – rewrite their essay now they are aware what constitutes an A grade answer for this particular exam question. The two A grade answers are added to the 'Best answers' display board. The pupils who wrote A grade essays are given a different wider reading task linked to the essay question.

The tweak

Pupils redo a piece of work after receiving feedback rather than moving onto something new.

Getting pupils to rank their group's work is a challenging activity because they need to have a very good understanding of the exam mark scheme and be able to notice subtle differences in each other's work. For example, in this lesson, there are two examples of A grade answers but the teacher asks his pupils to drill down deeper and make a judgement on which one would receive the most marks in the exam. The pupils are required to discuss at length the strengths and weaknesses of their own essay in order to decide on the correct ranking. Talking transparently about their work is key to creating a culture of excellence. Teachers shouldn't mistake this task as being about competition because it involves ranking; it is a chance for pupils to have mature conversations about whether their work truly is excellent. Reading better essays than their own and then rewriting their first essay attempt to turn it into an A grade answer, encourages pupils to aim for excellence.

Commitment to learning

Ability to listen to and learn from their peers

As mentioned previously in the chapter on Questioning (chapter 3, page 43), listening to and learning from your peers is not as easy as it seems. For pupils to become good listeners and talkers, we need to spend time explicitly teaching them how to do this. The task becomes even more complex when the content being discussed is each other's work; pupils can be sensitive about something they have produced. The challenge is not only to get pupils to accept feedback from their peers but also to actively seek out feedback opportunities. Pupils learning from each other has a relatively high effect size of 0.55 according to John Hattie (Hattie, 2009) so it is certainly worth considering in your planning how to support pupils in learning how to listen to and learn from each other.

Teachers have become experts at carefully designing success criteria for content-based tasks in order to make our expectations clear, but we can easily forget to teach pupils what we mean when we ask them to listen or discuss. For pupils to become good listeners and talkers, we need to spend some time explicitly teaching them how to do this: What would we see, hear and feel if someone was speaking or listening effectively?

Plenary prefects
Shaun Allison (classteaching.wordpress.com) 22 March 2013.

So, what are learning spies?
David Didau (learningspy.co.uk) 11 July 2011.

Significant and legitimate silence
Jennifer Ludgate (littlemisslud.wordpress.com) 7 February 2013.

Lesson snippet 1

Lesson context: Year 12 Philosophy and ethics, mixed ability class

Each pupil is given a different stimulus to read about the topic, 'tolerance'. The teacher shares the debate question for the lesson: 'Should a liberal society tolerate religious minorities?' The teacher gives the pupils 15 minutes to read their stimulus and take notes using a maximum of five bullet points. The pupils are told they will need to make use of what they have read but will only be able to use their bullet points. The pupils are sitting in a horseshoe layout so everyone can see each other; the teacher selects the first pupil to come to the front and share what they have learnt for two minutes. Whilst the pupil is speaking, no one is allowed to take notes; they can only listen. The teacher then gives the pupils an additional minute to make any notes they think will be useful in responding to the debate question. Once all pupils have spoken for two minutes and collated their notes, each pupil is given an A3 piece of paper on which they write one paragraph which sums up what they think. Pupils are then asked to place themselves along a continuum line depending on whether they think 'yes' or 'no'. The teacher questions the pupils to probe their thinking and challenge them to develop their arguments.

The tweak

Limit the amount of notes pupils can take when others are talking so they give their full attention to the speaker.

This is a tightly-structured task with the aim of pupils moving from having one idea to several ideas before connecting these ideas together to form their position on the debate question. All pupils contribute to this task which means that pupils are learning from each other. One issue that can arise when asking pupils to share information with each other is that they can end up copying their partner's work word for word and not really understanding what they're copying. The pupil begins the lesson with only five bullet points; already they have to be selective in what information they think will be most useful. Coupled with this, the teacher does not allow pupils to take any notes when a pupil is talking; this may seem counterproductive but it forces the pupils to listen much more carefully if they cannot write it down. By making the pupils wait until the pupil has finished talking, they need to piece together the new information they have heard and consider how it changes what they were thinking previously. Using a continuum line helps the pupils to consider the subtleties of the debate question – there clearly isn't a simple 'yes' or 'no' response (you'd hope not in a Philosophy class!) and this strategy visibly emphasises this to the pupils.

Lesson snippet 2

Lesson context: Year 9 Drama, mixed ability class

Pupils are working in groups of five to devise a performance based on the play *Blood brothers*. The task is to script and perform an alternative ending to the play, incorporating some of the dramatic techniques that the pupils have been experimenting with during the term. The script is written and the pupils are now working on turning the script into an engaging performance. The teacher asks the class: 'What knowledge and skills will effective groups have when making decisions about their performance?' Each group is given a few minutes to discuss some of the dramatic techniques they have learnt, specific content from the original play source as well as important group skills. The teacher chooses one pupil from each group to step out of the discussion and become an observer. The teacher gives each observer a clipboard with a blank grid with question prompts to help the observers take notes. The questions are: 'What dramatic techniques are discussed by the group and do they justify why they choose particular techniques to use?' 'Do all members of the group use their knowledge of the play when considering how to stage their performance?' 'How does the group make decisions and are they good decisions?' Based on what you have seen and heard from your group, what one piece of advice are you going to give your group? Observers take notes for 15 minutes before the teacher stops the pupils and asks the observers to provide feedback to their groups before continuing with their work.

The tweak

Pupils observe their peers learning and give feedback on what they have noticed.

Effective group work is notoriously difficult to get right! As a teacher, it is hard to judge if all pupils are pulling their weight and if they are all working towards a common goal. In the past, there has been a lot of pressure put on teachers to make sure their pupils are working in groups; however, our belief is that pupils should only work in groups if the outcome of the task could not be achieved with similar results by working individually. We need to ask ourselves: 'What are they getting out of this task academically and not just socially?' In this lesson, it is clear that group work is necessary. The teacher has used pupil observers to help the groups reflect on how they are working together and whether they are making good use of what they have learnt during the term. Setting up pupil observers is an effective strategy that teachers can use to get an accurate picture of what is really going on in their classroom. Pupils need to be able to listen to their observer's feedback and think about their own contributions. Since the observer is part of the group, it is in their best interest to ensure that they take their role seriously because they have an opportunity to influence the group's decision making.

Lesson snippet 3

Lesson context: Year 10 Spanish, middle ability class

Pupils have been set homework in the previous lesson to find out new vocabulary for the topic, 'the environment'. The teacher had split the class in half, labelling pupils A or B. Each half of the class was given different vocabulary to learn for their homework. This lesson, the teacher explains that 'A' pupils will teach 'B' pupils the new vocabulary they have learnt and then they will swap over. At the start of the lesson, the teacher displays an extract about global warming on the board; the extract features numerous words which pupils were asked to find out for homework. Pupils will only be able to translate the extract once they know the meaning of all of the new vocabulary. Pupils get into pairs based on the letter they were labelled with in the previous lesson. The teacher asks pupils to write their new vocabulary onto a mini whiteboard to enable her to check who has done their homework. Those pupils who have not done their homework will sit out this task and be given a dictionary to complete the translation task and be sanctioned in line with school policy. The teacher sets a timer for 60 seconds; pupil A has 60 seconds to share their vocabulary with pupil B. The timer is then reset so pupil B can share with pupil A. All pupils then reread the extract on the board and begin to translate it into English before answering a series of comprehension questions. During the time the pupils are translating the extract, the teacher intervenes with pupils who need extra support with translation.

The tweak

Pupils are given different homework which they can then teach to their peers.

One of the problems all teachers face is the dreaded moment in class when you ask pupils for their homework and some of them haven't done it. You need to sanction the pupils if they haven't completed their homework but you also want to increase pupils' sense of agency. In this example, the teacher has made a decision about how they are going to use homework as a way of making pupils more responsible. In her class, there are two types of homework and the pupils are used to the routine of receiving either an extended piece to be marked by the teacher or a shorter vocabulary-building task that will be used in class. Her pupils know that if they do not do their shorter vocabulary homework, it will be picked up straight away during the timed activity pair share, since they will have nothing to say! This is embarrassing for pupils so they quickly realise it is easier to do the homework, plus they don't want to let down their peers. The teacher is firm but fair in her decision to remove pupils from the task who have not done their homework. By not showing commitment to their work, those pupils will have to work by themselves with only a dictionary for support rather than learning from their peers and helping each other.

Annotated Art and design lesson plan

Teacher	Date and period	Subject	Class and ability range	Boy:girl ratio
Mr Gould	02/02/P5	Art and design	Y9 Mixed ability	15: 12

Student context:	EAL	SEN	G&T
	1	SPLD: 2 MLD: 2 BESD: 3	1

Learning objective	Differentiated learning outcomes
Develop technical knowledge and skills by manipulating the qualities of paint to meet the target you set for the lesson.	1. Develop and use technical knowledge and skill to realise intentions, using the qualities of paint and the formal elements effectively. 2. Demonstrate confident understanding of the use of paint to realise your intentions. 3. Exploit the potential of paint independently to make intuitive and analytical judgements to develop and realise intentions.

Resources needed
Interactive whiteboard presentation, fine paintbrushes, water pots, paint palettes, viewfinders.
Support sheet for assessment - key words and sentence structure, named lollipop sticks for questioning.
Traffic light cards, project checklist.

> Pupils are spending a significant amount of time working independently on an extended project. This initial reflection reminds pupils what they have learnt so far and the context of the lesson in relation to previous and future lessons.

Lesson content	Planned opportunities to check prior knowledge and further pupil progress
Hook Recap on current stage of the project referring to key words, processes and artists. Peer assessment - pupils will be asked to fill in an assessment sheet for someone else's painting in the class listing two WWW's (what went well) and one EBI (even better if) to help the individual improve their work.	Questioning at the start about what we have been looking at and the processes we have been using to get to our final outcome. How have these helped us? Peer assessment - pupils to provide constructive advice to another pupil in the class to help them improve their painting.
New learning activities Pupils will then swap back their work and read the constructive piece of advice that they have been given. Once individuals have read through the comments they will then write their own target for the lesson and will use this as their focus for the lesson.	Pupils to individually set their target for the lesson by using their peer's comments to help them.
Reflection activities Exit cards will be used for pupils to reflect on what they have learnt in the lesson, referring to the learning objectives set at the beginning of the lesson. An example of this will be on the board. These will be handed to pupils at the end of the lesson.	Pupils will respond to the target they set themselves using the exit card to self-assess what they did to meet the target and what they could have been done better to meet their target.

> There is a 'reflect and refine' culture in this class. Pupils reflect on where and how they have made progress and set themselves and each other targets to move forwards.

> There is regular use of exemplar answers, model work and directing pupils to look for a specific aspect in another pupil's work which encourages pupils use these examples to take more risks and be more creative.

This strategy encourages participation as pupils need to keep focused in case they are randomly picked next (particularly if the sticks are sometimes replaced to avoid pupils switching off once they have answered)!

Allows pupils to work independently but to ask for help when needed in a less threatening way.

Differentiation strategies used in the lesson	Through task	Through questioning all stages	Through groupings	Through teacher and other adults' support
S – Starter NL – New learning activity R – Reflection activity T – Throughout	NL – Lesson objectives differentiated. This enables lower ability pupils to achieve and G&T pupils to remain challenged.	S, NL and T – Pupils will be targeted in relation to SEN data to ensure they have full understanding.	T – Use of seating plan in the classroom to increase pupil progress in relation to SEN and EAL data on tracking sheet.	T – The use of traffic light cards will enable the teacher to identify pupils who need additional support.
	R – Lower ability pupils will be able to use the key words and sentence structure suggestions sheet to enable them to develop constructive targets in the form of WWW and EBI.	S, NL, T – Lollipop sticks will be used to select pupils randomly for questioning.

T – Each pair will be given traffic light cards to enable their progress to be assessed within the lesson. | T – Each pair of pupils will be given traffic light cards to enable their progress to be assessed within the lesson. Pupils will be encouraged to support one another prior to needing the teachers intervention. | T – SEN and EAL pupils will be supported according to the teaching strategies on their individual IEPS's. |

Literacy/numeracy links
Key terms displayed on board.
Key word lists given out to pupils.
Pupils have a version of the learning outcomes in more accessible language that they constructed with the teacher in a previous lesson.
Reference to ratio in relation to mixing a range of tones.
Scale and proportion in relation to the grid technique.

Homework task
Develop your use of tone through colour by layering colouring pencils to create a tonal drawing from a section of your Photoshop portrait.

The teacher has carefully planned the project so that pupils can complete meaningful and accessible homework each week. The homework ensures pupils reflect on their classwork and complete practical activities.

The teacher asks questions and suggests where they should look at other pupil's work for inspiration rather than telling the pupil what to do.

Commitment to learning provision in Art and design lesson plan

- The language of the learning objective and outcomes is challenging, so the pupils speak in terms of the objective. Differentiated outcomes have been written by the pupils and are always on display (pupils are reminded to get these from their books at the start of the lesson).

- The initial reflection reminds pupils what they have learnt so far and the context of this lesson in relation to previous and future lessons. This is particularly important for project-based learning, as pupils will spend a significant portion of the lesson working independently, so need to keep track of what they have achieved and what their next steps will be.

- Peer and self-assessment are well embedded. Pupils understand the process; there are good procedures in place and the discussion is meaningful.

- There is a 'reflect and refine' culture in this class. Pupils reflect on where and how they have made progress and set themselves and each other targets to move forward.

- The teacher intervenes when pupils are really stuck (when they show their red traffic light card). The teacher does not provide answers but asks questions and suggests where they should look at another pupil's work for inspiration.

Missed opportunities and tweaks

Missed opportunity

The project has been set up by the teacher, with the project checklist provided for pupils. This means that all pupils will follow the same or a similar project plan and will make limited decisions.

The tweak

Pupils can start a project by making their own project plan. This is not easy, but if you provide support such as an exemplar plan for another project, the level criteria that applies to this project and some overall objectives, this enables pupils to try for themselves. You can then offer more support if they feel they need it, for example a sheet of questions to guide them through their plan.

Missed opportunity

There is an extended portion of the lesson where pupils are working independently. This is a good thing but some pupils may lose focus and go off task, whereas others can become irritated when the teacher interrupts their artistic flow at a critical point.

The tweak

To feel confident that pupils are making very good progress when they are left to get on with it for extended periods of time, pit stop plenaries are very effective. These are particularly useful because they can be set up as a pause rather than interrupting your pupils' flow. You could ask pupils to take a pit stop in five minutes time so individuals can decide an appropriate point to reflect without it getting in the way of their work. You could also plan an optional pit stop so pupils can pause and reflect if they feel they need to.

Missed opportunity

The homework is set by the teacher and is the same for every pupil, regardless of their level or what they have achieved in the lesson.

The tweak

When working on a project that your pupils have been involved in planning, ask the pupils to set their own homework towards the end of a lesson. If exit cards are used, add a section for 'What I will do for homework' so that you can collect them in and monitor what pupils decide to set themselves.

In summary. . .

In this example, the teacher has organised her planning so that the class consider their art lessons as a continuum rather than stand-alone events. This project-based approach is an excellent starting point to develop more independent and committed learners. The next steps would be to plan to give more control of the learning over to the pupils and to offer further opportunities for the pupils to make their own decisions. If you take a project-based approach, you should ensure your planning builds in time for reflection and refinement throughout the project. It is also important to consider whether there is sufficient differentiation to stretch and challenge your pupils whilst providing adequate support.

Annotated Religious education lesson plan

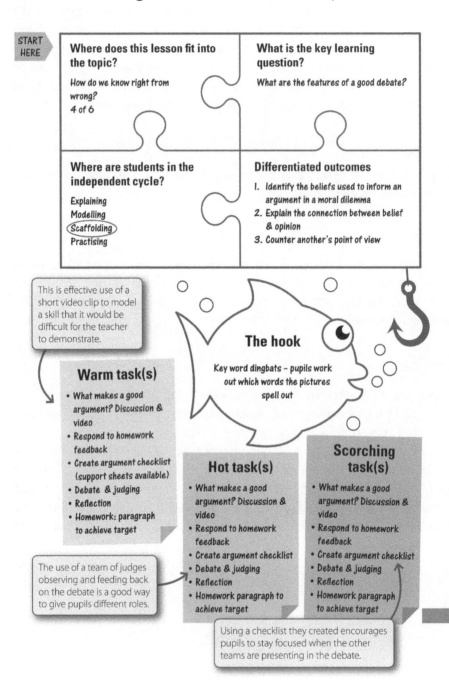

START HERE

Where does this lesson fit into the topic?

How do we know right from wrong?
4 of 6

What is the key learning question?

What are the features of a good debate?

Where are students in the independent cycle?

Explaining
Modelling
Scaffolding
Practising

Differentiated outcomes

1. Identify the beliefs used to inform an argument in a moral dilemma
2. Explain the connection between belief & opinion
3. Counter another's point of view

This is effective use of a short video clip to model a skill that it would be difficult for the teacher to demonstrate.

The hook

Key word dingbats – pupils work out which words the pictures spell out

Warm task(s)

- What makes a good argument? Discussion & video
- Respond to homework feedback
- Create argument checklist (support sheets available)
- Debate & judging
- Reflection
- Homework: paragraph to achieve target

Hot task(s)

- What makes a good argument? Discussion & video
- Respond to homework feedback
- Create argument checklist
- Debate & judging
- Reflection
- Homework paragraph to achieve target

Scorching task(s)

- What makes a good argument? Discussion & video
- Respond to homework feedback
- Create argument checklist
- Debate & judging
- Reflection
- Homework paragraph to achieve target

The use of a team of judges observing and feeding back on the debate is a good way to give pupils different roles.

Using a checklist they created encourages pupils to stay focused when the other teams are presenting in the debate.

Monitoring progress points

1. Pupils respond to written feedback from T

2. T reads speech checklist

3. Peer assessment of arguments

4. T collects exit tickets

This reflection time makes feedback much more meaningful and helps pupils plan how they can move their learning forward.

There is a well-established routine of working in different groups, including talk pairs, writing pairs and debate teams and these groups have pupils matched according to ability for a specific skill.

Groupings

Individual
• Response to marked work
• Reflection task (Your learning outcome)

Pair
• Hook & discussion in 'talk pairs'
• 'Writing pairs' for speech checklist

Group
• Debate in team of 4 with one team of judges

Key words

Persuasive
Proposition
Opposition
Argument
Floor
Motion
Debate

A simple way for the teacher to collect information on the progress of each pupil to inform future planning.

Questions to develop thinking

What makes R's argument persuasive?
How could you oppose K's argument?

The takeaway

Pupils complete an exit ticket giving their answer to the key question.

Commitment to learning provision in Religious education lesson plan

- One of the most striking aspects of this lesson plan is how the pupils are expected to work in a range of different groups. Pupils are asked to work in 'talk pairs', 'writing pairs' and 'debate teams'. It is clear that the teacher has matched pupils according to ability in their writing and debating groupings and in differing ability for their talking pair.

- Having a key learning question in place of a learning objective means it is simple to understand what is expected of pupils during the lesson. It also makes the 'identify your own learning outcome' reflection task more straightforward as pupils can think about what they have done that shows they can answer the question.

- The plan includes dedicated time for pupils to read the teacher's feedback on their written work and decide on their next steps. The homework task then gives pupils an opportunity to meet the target they have been set. This means pupils are not just engaging with their target but also doing a piece of work almost immediately to try and meet their target.

- The task to create a checklist for argument speeches has many good aspects to it. Firstly, pupils of different abilities discuss their ideas before making the checklist, so pupils that are less confident can talk through their ideas before writing. Secondly, the teacher can use the checklist (during the lesson and when it is taken in at the end) to assess pupils' progress in understanding the features of a good argument. Finally, pupils use their checklist to assess their peers, so they are more likely to stay focused when the other groups are presenting.

- The debate activity is well organised, with 'teams' arranged in the previous lesson.

- The use of one team of judges (the judges are rotated for each debate) means that pupils take on different roles. Being forced to just observe and not get involved in the debate gives pupils a different perspective.

Missed opportunities and tweaks

Missed opportunity

The main downside is that the teacher will lead the majority of the lesson and consequently have very little time to check on individual progress or ask challenging questions.

The tweak

You could plan for a debate to be led by a pupil or small group of pupils. You could make this part of the role of the judging group and they could also be given feedback (and a score) on how well they performed their role. Obviously, it is important to agree the rules on leading a debate with your pupils and if you feel brave, the leading pupils could be given the authority to sanction or reward the other pupils in the class as appropriate. To make this activity more fun, you could buy an inflatable hammer for the debate leaders to demand 'order'!

Missed opportunity

The peer questioning during the debate is ad hoc – pupils are asked if they have a question for the team that has just presented. In such a situation, the same pupils will keep putting their hands up to ask a question and many won't participate.

The tweak

It is easy to forget to build time in your planning for pupils to ask questions between themselves, but this can be the best part of a lesson. It may be that you plan extra time for activities such as a debate so that there is sufficient time for peer-to-peer challenge questions. It is also important that you prepare all pupils to question their colleagues, so you could use a random name generator to select who asks the questions or give out question stem cards (for example, 'If it was up to me, I would. . .' or, 'I hear what you're saying but what about. . .') to pupils of a range of levels to achieve this.

Missed opportunity

The use of pupil-designed checklists should keep pupils engaged throughout presentations but some may lose focus as more teams present. This means the third and fourth team have a harder time presenting, which is unfair.

The tweak

Adding a measurable element of competition can often motivate pupils to rise to the challenge, both when presenting and scoring their peers. You could add a scoring system agreed by the pupils and adapt the roles of the judges; perhaps each judge could be asked to focus and give feedback on a particular aspect for each group's presentation.

In summary. . .

A debate is a very difficult activity to organise, so ensure your planning includes provision of support and opportunities for pupils to take the lead so they are more involved in the process. Adding an element of real competition will also encourage independence. This exemplar plan is an ambitious lesson plan in terms of timing. There is a lot to get through but by investing time to establish the routines of working in different groups and by using a timer to maintain pace, you can make this type of lesson achievable.

Top tweaks checklist: commitment to learning

- Provide exemplar plans for pupils to use to help them create their own plans for independent projects.

- Plan several 'pit stop' plenaries for when pupils are being left to get on with it to ensure you are aware of the progress they are making and to keep them on track.

- Trust pupils to set their own homework, giving them clear parameters through criteria that must be met or through a choice of tasks, towards the end of a lesson to develop a sense of autonomy and responsibility in the pupils.

- Encourage pupils to build their confidence in leading feedback sessions by allowing them to give out rewards and sanctions to their peers, in the same way you would as the teacher.

- Use a range of feedback strategies to monitor the progress pupils have made working by themselves or in a group, such as: asking different groups to feedback on different aspects; sharing feedback between groups by doing 'pairs to fours' or 'home and away tables' or randomly selecting pupils after listening to their peers' feedback to ask questions as devil's advocates.

- Ensure there is a good balance between teacher talk and pupil talk so that pupils can become more independent by questioning each other and not relying as much on the input of the teacher.

- Add a measurable element of competition to motivate pupils to rise to the challenge that is being offered to them; encourage them to complete a more challenging task, assuring them that it is ok to be unsuccessful sometimes – as long as you learn where you went wrong and what you can do differently next time.

- Develop a bank of window pit stops as a group and ask each member of staff to choose three to try out for a term. Window pit stops are activities that require pupils to reflect in some way on their learning so far, but are set up to be completed during a progress window of 10 to 15 minutes as decided by the pupil. They may decide to try the same three out with all their classes or they may select two or three for each class if they decide certain pit stops would be more suitable for a particular class or age range.

- Try out different ways to gather feedback from groups during staff training to demonstrate how this could be varied in lessons. Examples could include: taking feedback on a different aspect of an activity from each group; pupils having to build on feedback from another group by asking a question or challenging something that has been said; groups providing feedback to each other by mixing up groups (for example: using pairs to fours, home and away or colour to rainbow groups) or setting up the task so groups contribute different aspects, either by 'jigsawing' where each group contributes something that contributes to the bigger picture or through 'graffiti walls' which are pieces of sugar paper given out to groups, each focusing on a particular aspect of the topic. For further discussion of group work strategies see the National Strategy publication 'Pedagogy and Practice: Teaching and Learning in Secondary Schools Unit 10: Group work' available via the link http://webarchive.nationalarchives.gov.uk/20110809101133/http://wsassets.s3.amazonaws.com/ws/nso/pdf/100963eeb bb37c81ada6214ed97be548.pdf

- Many members of staff may have tried out role cards (see online resources and appendix 4), which specify the responsibilities for different pupils within a group (for example: group leader, scribe, and questioner). These cards encourage group work by ensuring every pupil knows that they have certain expectations within their group. If your staff have never used role cards you could show some examples and ask them to consider the different roles that could be used in their subject. To take this a step further, ask staff members to make role cards for their subject but to consider firstly the different roles that may be required for different types of task (written, verbal, practical) and secondly to consider for each role both the core and additional responsibilities. The additional responsibilities would be those that would normally go on a role card whereas core responsibilities would be those that every pupil is expected to fulfil. This overcomes the problem that sometimes occurs when roles are assigned which is that certain pupils will sit back when they have done their bit. Core responsibilities could include things such as,

'Write a summary of the key points discussed by your group,' or 'Ensure all equipment is packed away properly at the end of the task'.

- Create a bank of short video clips showing teachers modelling to pupils. These can be used in training sessions, or can be shared with teachers or teaching assistants to give them some ideas that they can apply to their own practice. The modelling process does not need to be perfect; if a teacher makes mistakes it can be better for pupils to see, so long as the teacher identifies the errors and talks through them.

- Run a session with your department or faculty in which teachers create a list of techniques or concepts that pupils often need to be shown or have explained to them many times. Allocate the techniques and concepts from the list to different members of staff and ask them to find videos online, create their own or ask pupils to create videos on their specified topic. The department could use them within lessons, as 'flipped learning' (a technique whereby pupils watch videos in advance of the lesson and apply what they learn from these in a lesson to complete tasks such as exam questions, debates or extended writing) resources or for teaching assistants to watch before a lesson (teaching assistants are often keen to be more prepared for lessons in advance but have very little planning time. A video would be a simple and fast way to be one step ahead and better able to support pupils).

- Suggested staff enquiry questions for developing commitment to learning could include, 'Which strategies are effective in ensuring all pupils participate in group tasks?' or 'How can I best monitor progress without interrupting learning for my GCSE class?'

6 Marking and feedback

(Not to be confused with ticks, stickers and telling the pupils, 'Well done!')

Our final chapter is on the biggest challenge of all: marking and feedback. Strictly speaking, marking pupils' work is not the same as planning a lesson, yet we would argue that it is nigh on impossible to plan effective lessons if you are not carrying out high-quality marking. Therefore, we have included this chapter because we want to share with you different approaches to marking. There is no one-size-fits-all approach to marking; we definitely advocate using a range of strategies from your marking repertoire at different points in the year. If you try and mark all of your pupils' work from every class all at the same time, you will end up burning out. Instead, plan ahead which pieces will be marked in detail and which pieces will be marked more quickly or with a small, specific focus. The most important thing you can do is to explain to your pupils what your strategies are so that they understand how to get the most from your marking.

Without doubt, with every academic year that has passed since our PGCE, we have got better at planning lesson sequences and adapting existing schemes of work. We have become more discerning about what we think works for us and our pupils, making decisions that are informed by reading a considerable amount of books and academic papers. Each year, we keep what has worked and tweak things that aren't working as well as we'd hoped.

Yet one thing that still remains unbelievably tricky is marking pupils' work. It should be simple. You teach some lessons; you plan some learning outcomes; you test whether pupils have learnt something; you give them feedback; they improve – hurrah! But there's always this nagging feeling that if only we'd marked more often, in more depth, then the pupils would have made more progress. We always start off with the right intentions but – come January – we are on our knees, drowning in the endless books to mark and get back before the next lesson.

The whole concept of marking has changed dramatically since we started teaching. When we started as NQTs, it was ok to 'tick and flick' most of the work as long as you properly assessed the end of unit test (which normally took place about every half term). A couple of years later, we started giving comments which identified what the pupils had learnt and highlighted areas for improvement. Fast-forward another couple of years and this turned into the WWW/EBI acronym, which our line managers searched for evidence of in our books. In more recent times, another layer has been added to the marking where we now identify an action that the pupils must take to address their EBI target and line managers now look for evidence of pupil response as well as our original feedback.

We're not suggesting for one minute that these developments aren't positive; we believe wholeheartedly that our marking was pretty mediocre at the beginning and is now so much better because it is encouraging pupils to take on board their strengths and weaknesses and commit to making improvements. Nonetheless, it would be a lie to say that these changes haven't led to a massive increase in workload. As a result, we have had to think much more carefully and strategically about our marking and feedback across the year if we are to stay on top of it.

Seminal research from Professor John Hattie in his book *Visible learning* (Hattie, 2009) and the follow-up *Visible learning for teachers* (Hattie, 2012) states that feedback has a very high effect size (0.73) in terms of pupils making better than expected progress. This shouldn't come as too much of a surprise because many teachers are all too aware of the powers of formative assessment if they have read *Inside the black box* (Black and Wiliam, 2001). What makes Hattie's work so compelling is it is based upon the findings of over 900 research studies.

It is only recently that we've learnt that just because one approach to marking worked well with one class does not mean it will work with another class. You need a few marking approaches up your sleeve and to use your professional judgement to decide which ones will work for you, with your classes and in your context. We've all got different school marking policies – some more regimented than others – so we're not going to claim in this chapter that we have the answer that will make marking a breeze. What this chapter aims to do is to prompt you into questioning your approach to marking, reflect on the quality of the feedback you are giving to pupils and consider whether your feedback and the pupils' responses gives you a view of the progress made by pupils over time. We identify common problems that colleagues have shared with us and suggest tweaks to your marking practices.

Oh, and a note on progress. Real progress happens over time, not in 20 minute bite-sized chunks. You need to leave space in between what you've taught and when you test pupils' knowledge to see if they really have learnt something. If a teacher writes on the board an example of how to use a semicolon and then five minutes later the pupils write their sentences using a semicolon, does that mean they really know how to use a semicolon? Maybe. Maybe not. Can they use the semicolon accurately three weeks later? Now that is progress. The best way to measure pupils' progress is by looking at the dialogue that is created between teacher and pupil. What have you highlighted for the pupils as an area to work on? Have they made an improvement? Ten pages later, have they stopped making the same mistake? Quality teacher feedback followed by quality pupil response is the best indicator of long-term progress.

Later in this chapter, you will find discussions of a range of blogs detailing different approaches to marking the writers have explored with their pupils. These teachers are incredibly honest about the successes and the pit falls of their own marking journeys, which is what makes these blogs so valuable. We summarise the key ideas in each blog to show how you can tweak your marking and feedback to improve the progress of your pupils whilst maintaining a manageable workload.

Marking involves a considerable investment of time and effort for teachers and should be the same for pupils! It is important to spend time planning what, how and when you will mark in order to have the greatest possible impact. The four points discussed below will help you to consider how you can achieve this and the tweaks that follow suggest ways to overcome the challenges faced by teachers trying to maximise pupil progress through feedback.

1. Dealing with key pressure points in the school year

When you start the year, highlight on your calendar all of the key pressure points you will face in terms of your marking capacity. This will probably include controlled assessment deadlines, mock examinations and end of unit assessments. These dates are non-negotiable as they have already been set on the calendar. At these points in the year, you will have a heavy marking workload. This is when some classes start to suffer because you can't keep on top of what you've promised yourself and your pupils that you will mark. In times like these, think about how you will be able to make use of teacher and peer feedback that can take place during class time. For example, if you are marking extended written work for one class then plan an oral presentation you can assess in class or a multiple choice test for other classes you teach.

2. Deciding what to look for in your marking

Not all feedback will focus on the same things. There will be times when you might be looking out for your pupils' use of subject-specific vocabulary, or to see whether your class has mastered a particular concept, or you might be marking a lengthy assessment that covers more than one topic the pupils have been learning. Depending on your focus, this will influence which marking approach you decide to use (in the blogs that follow, there are a plethora of ideas that fit different marking purposes). Whatever approach you choose, it needs to be useful in helping the pupils to recognise whether they have met their learning goal and to identify what they need to do to close any learning gaps.

3. A common language for learning

A common language for learning is very helpful to pupils when they are looking to make improvements in their work. Some schools have this built into their marking and feedback policy. If your school doesn't, what language will you use? WWW/EBI? Target? DIRT task?

MRI? Action? These are some of the phrases we've come across. Consistency is essential. By all means, use different marking approaches to get the pupils to respond to your feedback but make sure that when you use a word or phrase, they will understand what you mean. Don't confuse pupils with too many acronyms that you use for a while and then move onto something new. We like to use 'strengths', 'gap' and 'action'.

4. Routines for pupils to act upon your feedback

After you have assessed your pupils' work, decide when they will act upon your feedback – remember that what might work for one class might not work for another. For example, if you have a challenging class, you may decide not to use homework as a time for them to act upon your feedback because they might not do it or they might need your input which they can't get at home. You may decide that there is a pattern emerging in the errors you've seen and you need to have a lesson where you will model whatever it is your pupils have not quite understood. You may decide that you will set aside half of the first lesson of each week for pupils to redraft or improve their work. Each class will require different routines.

Tweaking your marking and feedback planning

Read these blogs for some brilliant ideas on how to tweak your marking and feedback.

Problem

'I spend so long writing the same two or three comments on my pupils' work.'

The tweak

Use a taxonomy of errors as discussed by Kev Bartle (canonsbroadside.blogspot.co.uk, 'Using a 'Taxonomy of Errors' to Enhance Student Responses.' 3 May 2013).

This requires a teacher to think about the possible issues pupils might encounter when working on an assessed task. These are written onto a slide and categorised into beginner, intermediate and advanced errors. Instead of teachers writing out the targets in full, a number is assigned to each error in the taxonomy and is recorded for the pupils. There is an improvement task attached to each error.

Problem

'I work much harder than my pupils when it comes to marking. I don't think some of them even put in that much effort.'

The tweak

Use RAG (**r**ed, **a**mber **g**reen) self-assessment before marking as discussed by Kev Lister (kevs-variability-thoughts.blogspot.co.uk, 'RAG to clean up marking.' 23 November 2013) and Damian Benney (mrbenney.wordpress.com, 'My RAG123 marking experiment.' 16 January 2014).

Kev and Damian's approach to marking in their blogs is based on prioritising frequency of feedback and getting pupils involved in assessing their own progress. Pupils give themselves a red, amber or green rating based on how confident they are with what they have learnt and then give themselves 1, 2 or 3 for effort during class. When the teacher reads the pupils' work, the main function is to check whether the pupils' assessment of themselves is accurate. The teacher may pose questions for the pupils to consider in the next lesson or decide to reteach aspects of the lesson.

Problem

'My pupils are getting stuck and not making the progress I'm expecting. Their responses are too basic and lack detail.'

The tweak

Use SOLO taxonomy to make explicit to pupils how to develop more sophisticated knowledge and understanding as discussed by Andy Philip Day (meridianvale.wordpress.com, 'Planning for a SOLO performance in the Exam Hall.' 25 May 2013) and Stephen Tierney (leadinglearner.me, 'When Feedback Met Bloom.' 8 December 2013).

Andy is an advocate of using SOLO taxonomy to support pupils in talking about their progress. SOLO taxonomy stands for 'Structure of Observed Learning Outcomes'. He uses grids with the different stages of SOLO taxonomy, highlighting where he thinks his pupils have shown: uni-structural knowledge (one idea/point made); multi-structural (awareness of several ideas/points); relational knowledge (several connected ideas to form a bigger picture); or extended abstract knowledge (understanding something on a conceptual level so a pupil could apply the knowledge in a different context).

Stephen, like Andy, advocates SOLO taxonomy as a means of setting challenging learning outcomes and uses the concept of 'feedforward' (what actions will you take now?) alongside the more traditional feedback (what do you need to focus on?) This blog also looks at Bloom's taxonomy and breaks down knowledge into three types: factual, procedural and meta-cognitive. He looks at feedback and feedforward using these three types of knowledge. For example, factual feedback might be: 'You got three answers incorrect. Now find them and correct them.' whereas procedural feedback might be: 'You can use point, evidence explanation but you need to use more quotations.' Meta-cognitive feedback might ask the pupil to assess themselves first and then plan their next steps in order to move the work to the next grade.

Problem

'I know that marking my pupils' work is important but it takes up so much of my time. How can I mark effectively but also have a social life?!'

The tweak

Use triple impact marking to ensure the pupils are working harder than you as discussed by David Didau (learningspy.co.uk, 'Marking is an act of love.' 6 October 2013).

David firmly believes that marking is an act of love! He recognises that it takes time but that it is worth it. He continues by saying that marking is planning and that it is the best form of differentiation. If you've given quality feedback, then your pupils' needs have been catered for because you have identified what they need to focus on to improve and built in lesson time for them to make sure they make your suggested improvements. David shares five ideas he has about how to get the most out of your marking.

Problem

'I spend a lot of time marking but I'm not sure if it's really having an impact. How do I know if the strategies I use are effective in accelerating my pupils' progress?'

The tweak

Focus on making feedback stick by giving enough time over to getting pupils to reflect and act on your feedback as discussed by David Fawcett (reflectionsofmyteaching. blogspot.co.uk, 'Can I be that little bit better at . . . using methods to make feedback stick?' 2 November 2013).

David shares how several educational thinkers, including Berger, Hattie and Wiliam, have shaped his thinking on what he can do to make feedback stick. The blog draws upon research into what works and what doesn't. He discusses several strategies to encourage pupils to engage with their teacher's feedback and illustrates this with photographs of his pupils' work.

Problem

'I mark my pupils' work and identify where they are going wrong but even after they have corrected their mistakes, they make the same errors in the next piece.'

The tweak

View marking as an opportunity to make errors explicit and set up tasks where pupils have to close their knowledge gap as discussed by Tom Sherrington (headguruteacher.com,

'Making Feedback Count: "Close the Gap". 10 November 2012) and Chris Hildrew (chrishildrew. wordpress.com, 'Closing the Gap Marking – Twilight CPD.' 16 January 2014).

Tom views all quality marking as a means of 'closing the gap'. He believes that it is misguided to impose a certain way of marking on teachers; there is a menu of strategies and teachers need to use their professional judgement to work out what is best for them and their pupils. However, using the phrase 'closing the gap' with pupils, regardless of the method, teachers begin to change how they view marking. The onus is on the pupils to close the gap; the teachers provide the pupils with prompts, resources and time but the pupils realise it is their responsibility to address their areas for improvement.

Chris has led training for staff at his school on how teachers should use marking and feedback to close the learning gaps. The blog is rich in visual material; he includes the 'Prezi' he used for training staff as well as video clips from Berger and Wiliam to help illustrate his thinking. He ends by sharing 12 marking tips and considering the strengths and weaknesses of each method.

Problem

'I always start the year with good intentions about how I will mark my pupils' work more often, but by Christmas there's always one class which I've let slide because my exam classes are prioritised.'

The tweak

Mark little and often instead of waiting for the big assessment at the end of the topic as discussed by Joe Kirby (pragmaticreform.wordpress.com, 'What if you marked every book, every lesson?' 2 November 2013) and Harry Fletcher Wood (improvingteaching.co.uk, 'What if you marked every book, every lesson? Reinventing the feedback wheel.' 9 February 2014).

Joe and Harry set teachers a challenge by posing this question: what if we marked every book, every lesson? After an initial reaction of 'You must be mad!', Joe explores how a tight focus on precisely what you are marking, combined with codes and symbols as opposed to writing out the same targets several times, means this might just be possible. Harry sets a question for his class at the end of each lesson which they respond to; he collects in their responses and uses a red, orange or green dot to identify how well a pupil has understood the learning from the lesson. For each coloured dot, there is a specific activity to complete at the start of the next lesson.

Problem

'My marking is not a problem and my head of department says my books are fine but it's difficult to see how all of it is really making a difference to my pupils' progress.'

The tweak

Stop seeing marking as something you need to do to keep those higher up off your back; instead concentrate on creating a culture of continuous feedback from yourself and the pupils to see real learning gains as discussed by Alex Quigley (huntingenglish.com, 'Improving Written Feedback'. 16 June 2013).

Alex is an English teacher so has had his fair share of marking extended pieces of work over the years. Consequently, he has gathered together his best strategies and looks at how these strategies have helped him to improve the quality of his feedback. However, he shies away from quick fixes and states unequivocally that pupils need to be trained well if they are to respond to these approaches because they require greater input from them.

Top tweaks checklist: marking and feedback

- Produce an overview each term to identify assessments and reporting deadlines to help identify marking pressure points.
- Plan activities that will be quicker to mark when your marking load is heavier.
- Consider where your marking will focus on a specific aspect or skill.
- Build time into lessons and homework for pupils to read and respond to written feedback.
- Share exemplars and model how you expect pupils to respond to your written feedback.
- Use codes, target banks or a 'taxonomy of errors' to highlight common mistakes but avoid writing the same thing for many pupils.
- After marking a task in detail, plan follow-up activities that will enable pupils to 'close the gap' that has been identified in their work.
- Use peer and self assessment as a quality control stage before you provide teacher feedback.

Learning leader: marking and feedback

- Schools will have their own particular policies for scrutiny of pupils' work but it can also be a very useful departmental development activity. It may be that staff are asked to bring their books for a particular year group to look for examples of good marking and pupil responses, or staff could be given a copy of a piece of work that they all write feedback for and then compare this, or staff in a department could be paired up to mark a task to check consistency.

- A department may decide that their marking for a particular year group will focus on a specific aspect of pupils' work for a half term. Examples of this could be using semi-colons in English, different tenses in Spanish or a range of points of view in science, citizenship or history.

- Set staff a classroom-based task. Ask them to use their marking for a particular class to identify a key concept or skill that they need to re-teach the whole class. They then need to re-teach and design a task that they will give pupils after re-teaching to assess their understanding.

- Another classroom-based task to give staff is live marking. This involves the teacher walking round the class and skim-reading work as pupils are completing a task. The teacher can use a simple code for pupils to improve their work as they go along: for example a '?' means identify what is incorrect; an 's' means check spelling and a 'w' means show your working.

- An effective use of departmental development time could be to work together to produce a taxonomy of errors (as mentioned earlier in this chapter) for each assessment task used by the department. This could be taken further if staff then design specific tasks that pupils will be given (in class or as homework) based on the area that their work lacked.

- Suggested staff enquiry questions for marking and feedback might be: 'Which strategies ensure my pupils respond effectively to written feedback?' or 'How can I use peer and self assessment to improve the quality of work submitted for teacher feedback?'

References

Introduction

Cladingbowl, M. (2014), 'Why I want to try inspecting without grading teaching in each individual lesson'. Ofsted. Accessed February 2014: webarchive.nationalarchives.gov.uk/20141124154759/http://www.ofsted.gov.uk/resources/why-i-want-try-inspecting-without-grading-teaching-each-individual-lesson

Coe, R., Cesare, A., Higgins, S., and Major, L. E., (2014), 'What makes great teaching? Review of the underpinning research'. Accessed February 2015: www.suttontrust.com/wp-content/uploads/2014/10/What-Makes-Great-Teaching-REPORT.pdf

Wiliam, D. Keynote speech: Specialist Schools and Academies Trust (SSAT) Conference, December 2012.

Chapter 1

Didau, D. (2013) Blogpost, accessed April 2015: www.learningspy.co.uk/featured/great-teaching-happens-in-cycles/

Lemov, D., Woolway, E., Yezzi, K. (2012), *Practice perfect: 42 rules for getting better at getting better.* San Francisco: Jossey Bass, p.40.

Morrison-McGill, R. Blogpost, accessed February 2015: teachertoolkit.me/the-5-minute-lesson-plan

Tierney, S. Blogpost, accessed February 2015:
leadinglearner.me/2015/02/07/pedagogy-and-student-behaviours-great-teaching

Chapter 2

Berger, R. (2003), *An ethic of excellence: Building a culture of craftsmanship with students,* Portsmouth, NH: Heinemann, p.94.

Black, P. and Wiliam, D. (1998), *Inside the black box: Raising standards through classroom assessment.* London NFER: Nelson.

Quigley, A. Blogpost, accessed February 2015: huntingenglish.com/2013/03/19/shared-writing-modelling-mastery

Chapter 3

Alexander, R. (2006), *Towards dialogic teaching: Rethinking classroom talk.* London: Dialogos.

Bloom, B.S. (1956), *Taxonomy of educational objectives: The classification of educational goals.* New York. David McKay company.

Further reading on Philosophy for Children: Lewis, L. and Chandley, N. (2012), *Philosophy for Children Through the Secondary Curriculum*. London: Continuum.

Ogle, D.M. (1986), 'KWL: A teaching model that develops active reading of expository text'. Reading Teacher 39, 564–570.

Sayers, J. Blogpost, accessed February 2015: sayersjohn.blogspot.co.uk/2013/01/questioning.html

Sinclair, J. and Coulthard, M. (1975), *Toward an Analysis of Discourse: the English used by Teachers and Pupils*. OUP.

Chapter 4

Bjork, R. A. (2013), 'Desirable difficulties perspective on learning'. In H. Pashler (Ed.), *Encyclopedia of the mind*. Thousand Oaks: Sage Publications p.242 and p.243

Education Endowment Foundation toolkit. Accessed February 2015: educationendowmentfoundation.org.uk/toolkit

Sherrington, T. Blogpost, accessed February 2015: headguruteacher.com/2013/01/31/great-lessons-3-challenge

Chapter 5

Berger, R. (2003), *An ethic of excellence: Building a culture of craftsmanship with students*. Portsmouth, NH: Heinemann, p.5.

Coe, R., Cesare, A., Higgins, S., and Major, L. E., (2014), 'What makes great teaching? Review of the underpinning research'. Accessed February 2015: www.suttontrust.com/wp-content/uploads/2014/10/What-Makes-Great-Teaching-REPORT.pdf

Dweck, C. (2006), *Mindset: The new psychology of success*. New York: Random House, p.40.

Hattie, J. (2009), *Visible learning: A synthesis of over 800 meta-analyses relating to achievement*. London: Routledge, p.297

Chapter 6

Black, P. and Wiliam D. (2001) Inside the black box: Raising standards through classroom assessment, London NFER, Nelson.

Hattie, J. (2009), *Visible learning: A synthesis of over 800 meta-analyses relating to achievement*. London: Routledge, p.297.

Hattie, J. (2012), *Visible learning for teachers: maximising impact on learning*. London: Routledge.

Appendix 1: Biology SOLO lesson exemplar

The table below demonstrates SOLO taxonomy as applied to a Biology topic. There are two lesson examples from a unit about drugs and disease. Under each heading is a description for pupils to select the closest match to their situation at the start of the lesson and a task to complete in order to progress to the next step. The thinking maps (HOT SOLO maps) referred to are graphic organisers designed by Pam Hook (www.pamhook.com) to help pupils organise their thoughts.

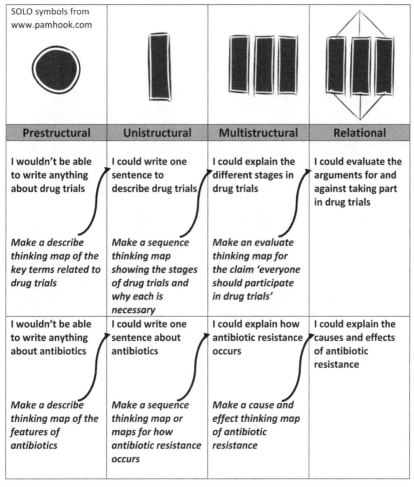

SOLO symbols from www.pamhook.com			
Prestructural	**Unistructural**	**Multistructural**	**Relational**
I wouldn't be able to write anything about drug trials	I could write one sentence to describe drug trials	I could explain the different stages in drug trials	I could evaluate the arguments for and against taking part in drug trials
Make a describe thinking map of the key terms related to drug trials	*Make a sequence thinking map showing the stages of drug trials and why each is necessary*	*Make an evaluate thinking map for the claim 'everyone should participate in drug trials'*	
I wouldn't be able to write anything about antibiotics	I could write one sentence about antibiotics	I could explain how antibiotic resistance occurs	I could explain the causes and effects of antibiotic resistance
Make a describe thinking map of the features of antibiotics	*Make a sequence thinking map or maps for how antibiotic resistance occurs*	*Make a cause and effect thinking map of antibiotic resistance*	

Appendix 2: Zones of learning target

There are many variations of this model online, however, our version below focuses on how learners may be feeling if they are in each 'learning zone'. This diagram has been very popular when we have used it in training with teachers and sparks a lot of thought and discussion. We have also used it with pupils; for example we show it on a slide to explain why it is important for them to feel challenged. Alternatively we use a poster sized version for pupils to add themselves to (on a sticky note), to show how they are feeling about the work in order to identify when the work is too easy or too challenging.

© Melanie Aberson and Debbie Light, 2015

Appendix 3: Revision action plan

Topic studied:	
Explain why mastering the knowledge in this topic is important for your studies.	
List between 2-5 specific aspects of the topic you found difficult. 1. 2. 3. 4. 5.	List a specific reason why you found each aspect of the topic difficult. 1. 2. 3. 4. 5.
Describe your behaviour in class when you found things difficult.	
List specific actions you carried out to help you whilst learning this topic when you found things difficult.	List specific actions that you haven't tried already which could help you develop your knowledge.
Decide the time and date of the six 20 minute time slots when you will improve your knowledge of this topic.	1. 2. 3. 4. 5. 6.

Appendix 4: Sample role cards

Front of cards:

Questioner It is your job to think about what are the important questions that need to be asked to understand the text	**Summariser** It is your job to listen to all the ideas and pull out the most important pieces of information
Noticer It is your job to think about what information is missing in the text and to notice if the text is biased in any way	**Scribe** It is your job to note down in bullet points the things you will discuss during feedback

Back of cards:

Summarisers: -Listen to all points of view -Can make decisions about what is most important	**Questioners:** -Listen to people's responses -Can read the text without too much difficulty
Scribes: -Can take notes quickly -Can speak out confidently in front of the class	**Noticers:** -Are curious about how language is used to manipulate -Can see things from different viewpoints

Subject index

Lesson snippets by subject

Art and design 30, 44, 72
Business studies 54, 95
Chemistry 81
Computing 29, 94
Design and technology 55, 99
Drama 104
Economics 101
English 22, 45, 70, 93
Food technology 23
Geography 26, 47, 75
German 52
Health and social care 73
History 76, 100
Maths 25, 48, 80, 97
Media arts 24, 53, 69
Music 27, 49
PE 21
Philosophy and ethics 103
Physics 96
Psychology 68
Religious education 28, 46, 74
Science 20, 50
Sociology 51, 92
Spanish 31, 77, 105
Sport 79

Full lesson plans by subject

Art and design 106–7
Business studies 82–3
Design and technology 56–7
English 60–1
History 32–3
Media arts 36–7
PE 86–7
Religious education 110–11
Science 14 and 16
Sociology 10 and 12

Index

ABC feedback 26
abstract thinking 21
action plans 97
assessment criteria 19, 27, 52
Assessment for Learning (AfL) 19–41
assessment objective (AO) 69, 84

blogs 1, 7, 26, 95, 118–19, 120–4
Bloom's taxonomy 51, 58, 64, 89, 121

challenging 2, 3, 7, 13, 15, 18, 19, 21, 25, 28, 29,
    40–1, 45, 46, 48, 49, 50, 53, 59, 63, 65, 67–90,
    92, 93, 98, 101, 108, 109, 113, 114, 121
checking understanding 47–9
choices 71–4, 90
collaborative learning 78–81
competition 15, 25, 70, 71, 91, 101, 113, 114
confidence 18, 39, 43, 50, 53, 54, 55, 58, 64, 81,
    84, 88, 89, 93, 94, 95, 112, 114
culture of excellence 98–101

data 3
dialogic teaching 43
differentiation 11, 13, 15, 18, 58, 84, 89, 108
discussion 18, 20, 21, 22, 24, 25, 26, 27, 38, 40,
    43, 44, 45, 46, 47, 48, 49, 53, 54, 59, 62–4, 65,
    69, 75, 77, 88, 90, 93, 97, 100, 101, 102, 104,
    108, 112
drafting 100

EBI (Even Better If) 26, 55, 117–18, 119
engaging 3, 15, 58, 64, 112
evaluating performance 88
exemplars 23–5, 41, 77, 84, 114, 124
exit cards/tickets 29, 109

feedback 19, 26–8, 38, 41, 73, 80, 95, 99–105,
    112, 114–15, 117–25
focus on learner 7
formal lesson plan 7–8, 10–13, 15, 36–7, 60–1,
    82–3, 106–7

games 49
Google Drive 79
groupings 13, 17, 18, 68–71, 84–5, 88–90, 112
growth mindset 91, 95–6

higher ability groups 50, 59, 77
hinge questions 65
homework 13, 73, 81, 84, 105, 109, 112, 114
hook 15, 58

independence, developing 75–8
independent learning 15, 91, 108
IRF (Initiation by teacher, Response by pupil,
    Feedback by teacher) 43

jigsaw section of lesson plan 15

key learning point 17, 18
key learning question 62, 112
key words 17
KWL (What do I know? What do I want to know?
    What have I learnt?) 52

language 28, 95
language for learning 119–20
league table 70
learning intentions 7, 19, 20, 22, 76
learning objectives 15, 18, 19–22, 34, 35, 40–1,
    62, 63, 108, 112
learning outcomes 11, 15, 18, 19–22, 23, 34,
    40–1, 59, 74, 76, 78, 84, 95, 104, 108, 112,
    117, 121
listening skills 31, 102–3
literacy 13
lower ability groups 44, 77, 97

marketplace format 81
marking criteria/scheme 21, 24, 28, 77, 101
marking planning 119–24
mind maps 76
mistakes, learning from 96
mixed ability groups 17, 29, 51, 59, 69–70, 84–5,
    88–9, 112
modelling 18, 23–5, 48, 75, 77, 97, 116
moderator feedback 41
monitoring progress 11, 17, 31, 85, 89, 112

numeracy 13

one page plan 7, 14–17, 32, 56–7, 86–7, 110–11
outstanding teachers 2–3

peer assessment/feedback 26–8, 34–5, 38–9, 55, 58–9, 99–105, 108, 112, 114, 119
peer observation 104
peer-to-peer questioning 53–5, 58–9, 113
Philosophy for Children 54
plenaries 11, 17, 53, 109, 114
practising 18
project-based approach/learning 74, 109

quality of teaching 2
questions 13, 17, 18, 30, 34, 41, 43–65, 74, 84, 89, 108, 112–14, 116

reflection 2, 11, 17, 18, 19, 30, 34, 50, 75, 108, 112, 122
resource planning/choosing 80, 85, 94
resources 13, 40, 41, 50, 52, 67, 72, 73, 74, 76, 80, 84–5, 89, 116, 123
reviewing learning/progress 29–31, 50–2
role play 55
roles, assigning 68
rules 63

scaffolding 18, 19, 45, 48, 49, 50, 72, 75
seating plans 69
social media 2
Socratic questioning 53, 62

Socrative 47
SOLO (structure of observed learning outcomes) taxonomy 21, 41, 121
speaking skills 31
stretch and challenge 67–90
stretch zone 93
success criteria 18, 34, 35, 39, 40–1, 77, 88, 99, 100
supporting pupils 3, 5, 13, 15, 18, 92

takeaway 17, 18, 29
target minimum grade (TMG) 38
taxonomy of errors 120
technology, using 23, 31, 47
template lesson plans 8–9
thinking questions 43–4
thinking task 75
training sessions 65, 90, 116

verbal feedback 28

WALT (we are learning to) 19
warm, hot, scorching model 72, 85, 89, 90
'What if?' questions 44
workstations 73
writing tasks 34–5, 51

zones of learning target 90